Data in
Sociology

Hugh Chignell

Causeway Press

Causeway Press Limited
P.O. Box 13
Ormskirk
Lancashire L39 5HP

British Library Cataloguing in Publication Data
Chignell, Hugh
        Data in sociology.
        1. Sociology
        I. Title
        301

        ISBN 0-946183-55-4

Typeset by Five Star Graphics, Liverpool
Printed and bound by The Alden Press, Oxford.

Contents

Author's Note
Earlier drafts of questions in this book have been tested with groups of students and have been adapted where necessary. I would welcome further comments from teachers and students and would be happy to offer advice and help on the use of *Data in Sociology*. Please write to me at Causeway Press.

Hugh Chignell

Page Design
Susan and Andrew Allen

Cover Design
Jeff Warwick Fineart

Typing
Ingrid Hamer

Acknowledgements
The author and publishers are grateful to all those who permitted the use of copyright material in this book. Due acknowledgement has been made to each source in the text. All HMSO sources are reproduced with the permission of the Controller of Her Majesty's Stationary Office, Crown copyright reserved. Items from the *Sunday Times* and the *Times Educational Supplement* with the permission of Times Newspapers Limited, ©1989. *Social Studies Review* is available only on subscription from Philip Allen Publishers Ltd, Market Place, Deddington, Oxford OX5 4SE (0869 38652). Cover picture is reproduced with the permission of the *Liverpool Daily Post and Echo*.

Every effort has been made to locate the copyright owners of material included. Any omissions brought to the publisher's notice are regretted and will be credited in subsequent printings.

Introduction

Answering Data Response Questions

For students who understand Sociology but just cannot write essays **data response questions** provide an opportunity to do well. For all students they test understanding of the subject in a different way from an essay; one which does not depend solely on having to remember facts. It is the ability to interpret, analyse and to judge the usefulness of data which is really important.

However, before attempting any of the questions in this book, there are two important points to remember:

1. Data response questions contain only **part** of the answer in the data. To understand and use that data you must bring to the questions your knowledge and understanding of the topic.

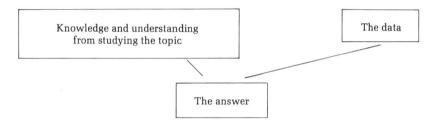

2. Because of this, a question can only be answered satisfactorily if the topic has been studied. For example, if you have not studied education, do not attempt a question on it, you will almost certainly do it badly.

WHAT'S IN A DATA RESPONSE QUESTION?

1. **Data Items**

   There are between three and five of these. They will have been chosen to represent a range of different types of sociological data. For example, they may include:
   - official statistics;
   - statistics gathered by a sociological researcher;
   - an extract from a book written by a sociologist;
   - part of a novel.

   The data will all refer to the same sociological issue or topic. Sometimes the content of items will be in **agreement**, so the theoretical ideas in one may be supported by other evidence. Sometimes there will be **disagreement**, which is more likely in sociology.

2. **Data Questions**

These follow the data items. There are four or five data questions. Each question will be awarded a certain number of marks, indicated in brackets, which will add up to a total of twenty-five. For some of the data questions, the answer will be contained in the data items, but others, scoring higher marks, will depend for their answers much more on the knowledge and understanding you already have.

READING AND ANSWERING THE QUESTIONS

You will probably get a lot of practice with data response questions and will develop your own approach to reading and answering them. Here are some suggestions which should help.

1. If you are doing a data response question in timed conditions you should be given **1 hour**. In that case you should spend about **10 minutes** reading the data carefully before looking at the data questions. Then read through the questions to get an idea of what you will have to do.

2. Make sure that you avoid a common mistake made by students. Do not write a very broad and general answer to a data question, so that when you go on to the next one you have already answered it. Careful reading of the data questions will prevent this from happening.

3. You can then work out roughly how long you need to spend on each data question. Simply multiply the marks for a question by two to give you the number of minutes to spend on that question:

   Example: 7 marks x 2 = 14 minutes.

4. Now read the first data question again and, thinking about it carefully, look at the data to which it refers. Write down rough notes for your answer. Put down any other evidence, sociological arguments or ideas which you want to introduce.

5. Keep an eye on the clock and when you feel reasonably confident then answer the first data question.

6. Work through all the data questions in the way described above.

READING STATISTICS

Quite a lot of these questions contain statistics, which will no doubt worry many students. Although they may contain a lot of figures, most statistics are very straightforward. If you remember the following hints and have enough practice, you should not have too much trouble answering them.

- Take time to read the tables **slowly**.
- Use a ruler if necessary to read down or across a line of figures.
- Look for the main **trends** (eg the increase in crime).
- Also look for major **differences** between social groups (eg male and female school subject choice).
- Look for 'blips' in trends over time (eg the divorce rate jumped after 1971).

- Use a calculator if you want to.
- Check to see if the figures are in thousands or percentages.
- Check on the date and source of the statistics.

Above all, do not be intimidated by sociological statistics. The only really difficult ones are on social mobility and no one understands those!

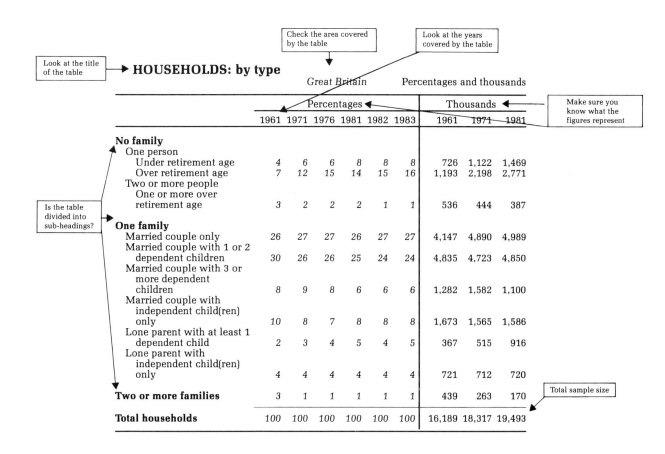

HOUSEHOLDS: by type

Great Britain   Percentages and thousands

	Percentages						Thousands		
	1961	1971	1976	1981	1982	1983	1961	1971	1981
No family									
One person									
Under retirement age	4	6	6	8	8	8	726	1,122	1,469
Over retirement age	7	12	15	14	15	16	1,193	2,198	2,771
Two or more people									
One or more over retirement age	3	2	2	2	1	1	536	444	387
One family									
Married couple only	26	27	27	26	27	27	4,147	4,890	4,989
Married couple with 1 or 2 dependent children	30	26	26	25	24	24	4,835	4,723	4,850
Married couple with 3 or more dependent children	8	9	8	6	6	6	1,282	1,582	1,100
Married couple with independent child(ren) only	10	8	7	8	8	8	1,673	1,565	1,586
Lone parent with at least 1 dependent child	2	3	4	5	4	5	367	515	916
Lone parent with independent child(ren) only	4	4	4	4	4	4	721	712	720
Two or more families	3	1	1	1	1	1	439	263	170
Total households	100	100	100	100	100	100	16,189	18,317	19,493

Look at the title of the table

Check the area covered by the table

Look at the years covered by the table

Make sure you know what the figures represent

Is the table divided into sub-headings?

Total sample size

VARIETIES OF DATA

When using a piece of data it is very important to look at where it comes from so that you can assess or judge that data as part of your answer, even if you are not directly asked to do so.

Examples:

ITEM A **PEOPLE IN HOUSEHOLDS: by type of household**

Great Britain				Percentages
	1961	1971	1981	1987
Type of household				
Living alone	3.9	6.3	8.0	9.9
Married couple, no children	17.8	19.3	19.5	21.5
Married couple with dependent children	52.2	51.7	47.4	44.1
Married couple with non-dependent children only	11.6	10.0	10.3	11.8
Lone parent with dependent children	2.5	3.5	5.8	4.7
Other households	12.0	9.2	9.0	8.0
All households	100	100	100	100

(*Social Trends 19*, HMSO, London, 1989)

Data Question: What do the statistics in Item A tell us about the changing structure of the modern family?

Comment: When you have explained what you think the figures tell us about modern family membership (for example, the growth of one-parent families), you can go on to evaluate the quality of the data. These are government statistics as the source 'HMSO' indicates. The categories, therefore, reflect government needs rather than sociological concerns. For example, the category of 'extended family' does not appear and the figures for those 'living alone' do not show co-habitation or those living in shared houses. Each year column is a 'snap-shot' and perhaps fails to show how individuals go through a life-cycle in which different household types are simply stages in their life rather than permanent arrangements.

ITEM B **PARENTHOOD**

So, one of the first things you notice in Northern cities hit by unemployment is babies, lots of babies, with very young parents: unemployed men in denims and trainers pushing buggies. The sight of teenage fathers is striking because it is in such stark contrast with the role of their own fathers, who weren't seen pushing prams when they were nineteen. You don't notice the young mothers so readily, because they're doing what they've always done. The real change is that many are doing it alone. Men come and go in their lives, but there is no necessary connection between motherhood and marriage. They are going it alone... because it is an alternative to aimless adolescence on the dole.

'Having a baby makes me feel a lot older and more mature. At first my mam and dad weren't pleased about me falling pregnant, and they used to go on about how I was going to manage. The bloke denied it was his, I felt awful though there's plenty have kids on their own round here.'

One of the women on this Sunderland estate told me they all recognised the drive:

'It's part of becoming a member of the community instead of just a reckless teenager. You don't need to get a job, when you're a mam. When you're a mam somebody **needs** you.'

(Beatrix Campbell *Wigan Pier Revisited: Poverty and Politics in the 80s,* Virago, London, 1984)

Data Question: What changes in the family are described in Item B?

Comment: The answer can make use of Beatrix Campbell's observations on young unemployed women in the North of England who have babies and so form one-parent families, but possibly within a larger community. A really good answer would perhaps go on to comment on the representativeness of Campbell's research. This data appears very 'journalistic' in its style; there is no suggestion of a sample or a survey which would be needed to confirm her findings.

As you should already know, official statistics are treated with a great deal of caution by sociologists, so if you refer to them, be prepared to be critical. Government reports, articles by journalists and parts of novels are often open to criticism for being 'biased' or 'subjective' even though they may give us useful insights into a sociological topic. Extracts from articles and books written by sociologists, including those from *Social Studies Review* and from Pat McNeill in *Society Today,* can also be judged, perhaps because of the perspective they employ or because they are out-of-date or in other ways not valid, reliable or representative.

THE PERFECT ANSWER

The advice so far is all very well but it does not actually tell you how to write a perfect answer. Most examiners are interested in testing students' ability or competence in three different areas of sociology:

1. **Knowledge and understanding** – What you know about sociology and how well you understand it.
2. **Interpretation and application** – Your ability to explain the data and use it to understand or explain something else.
3. **Evaluation** – How well you judge or assess the usefulness of evidence, a research method, a concept and so on.

Combined with all of these is your ability to express your answers clearly.

Because we know what examiners are looking for we have some important clues about how to answer the questions, and how not to answer them.

Here is an example of a typical data response question with suggestions for time allocation and an indication of what should be included in the answer:

Women and Waged Work

The Labour force is differentiated by gender, race and age. Those seeking labour are aware of these differences and may under certain economic conditions seek to exploit them. Disadvantaged groups may be much more likely to end up in secondary employment conditions, particularly if they are women or members of ethnic minorities. This has sometimes been explained by a theory known as the '**reserve army of labour**'. This theory argues that, given the tendency for economic conditions to change (from recession to boom, for example), employers may use those who for various reasons are not permanently in a job (women with small children, the unemployed) when they need more workers. When production drops again or the boom ends, they can then dispose of the temporary workers fairly easily. The difficulty with this theory is that it does not explain very well the contemporary patterns of employment for groups like women, in particular the fact they rarely do, even on a temporary basis, the same jobs as men.

(Adapted from Rosemary Deem, *Work, Unemployment and Leisure*, Routledge, London, 1988)

ITEM B **FEMALE EMPLOYED WORKFORCE**

Total, full-time and part-time participation rates: United Kingdom, 1984.

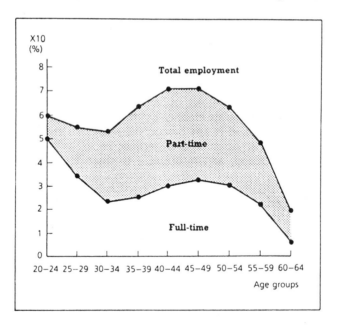

(A Dale and J Glover, 'Women's work patterns in the UK, France and the USA', in *Social Studies Review*, Vol. 3, No. 1, 1987)

ITEM C **EQUALITY OF JOB OPPORTUNITY**

The government is increasingly worried about the potential shortfall of young males in the workforce for the coming decade. So at last equality of job opportunity is being taken seriously. Demands are now being made for greater investment in the skills of women.

This is reflected in women's pay, which, according to the British Institute of Management, is rising more rapidly than men's.

Recent government legislation aims to prevent industry hindering the progress of women which is taken as evidence of its commitment to women.

Norman Fowler, the employment secretary, comments: 'In the 1990s, women will be playing a more and more important part in the labour market. It is vital to provide genuine equality of opportunity. Sex discrimination is not only unfair but harms the economy. Jobs should go to the best people, irrespective of sex.'

(Adapted from *The Sunday Times*, 29 January 1989)

Typical Data Questions	Marks	Time (mins)	Comments
1. Referring to Item A **explain** what is meant by the 'reserve army of labour'.	2	4	A typical **interpretation** question. The answer is in the data, but avoid copying. Some supporting evidence or example could be mentioned if you have time.
2. What are the advantages to employers of the existence of a 'reserve army of labour'?	2	4	Also an **interpretation** question. The basis for an answer is contained in Item A.
3. Briefly **explain** why women are more likely to be in the 'reserve army of labour' than men.	5	10	Part of the answer lies in the data. Both Items A and B can be used as well as your understanding from studying the topic.
4. **Describe** the pattern of female employment illustrated in Item B.	6	12	This is quite a difficult and unusual table which needs to be very carefully described. You will need to comment on the 'part time', 'full-time' and 'total employment' categories referring to both the percentage and age-group variables. Look also at the date and source of data.
5. **Illustrating** your answer with evidence from Item B, explain women's participation in part-time work.	4	8	The word **illustrate** means you should quote directly from the data. To **explain** you will need to suggest reasons why women's participation is as it is.

6. **Assess** the view in item C that 'in the 1990s, women will be playing a more and more important part in the labour market'.

6 12

Assess questions ask you to **judge** something (an 'evaluation' question). You will need to be very critical of the argument here, perhaps by using evidence from Items A and B and other knowledge you have. Criticise the 'source' of the view as well (a Conservative politician, quoted in a Conservative newspaper).

7. **Using evidence from here and elsewhere** examine the view in Item C that 'at last equality of job opportunity is being taken seriously'.

10 20

This is really a mini-essay. It will need a few minutes planning. You are clearly asked to use your wider **knowledge** as well as the data. You can also be critical of the source of the data as in the previous question.

Question 1 **Sociology and Education**

ITEM A **NON-PARTICIPANT OBSERVATION IN SCHOOLS**

Pat McNeill: Aren't teachers uncomfortable about having an outsider in their classroom?
Peter Woods (Open University researcher): Yes, and that is entirely understandable. But the effect depends on how you go about it. You have to develop a code of ethics and a feeling of mutual trust at an early stage. You have to remove the sense of threat you bring to the situation, the sort of threat that might be felt from inspectors or advisers. You have to reassure them about the purposes of your research, the means you will employ and the uses to which the research will be put...

PM: How does the presence of the researcher affect the children?
PW: That varies by age... Older students, by the time they are fourteen or fifteen, don't intrude in the same way as seven year olds when you are observing a classroom, but in other settings they will talk to you about their perspectives and ideas. Occasionally in the classroom they may draw your attention to some aspect of the interaction that illustrates a point they have made outside. All of this is interesting and usable material.

PM: So it is possible, with experience, to become confident that the account you are giving is a valid one.
PW: You hope so. This is where the qualitative method scores very highly. You are trying to understand what is going on in this particular piece of interaction, what are the underlying rules of behaviour in it. These may not be the same as the manifest rules. They may have been developed over a long period, through subtle forms of negotiation that people are not able to articulate but which an observer can extrapolate from the situation.

(Pat McNeill, 'Researching in Schools', *New Statesman and Society*, 24 June 1988)

ITEM B **FLANDERS' INTERACTION ANALYSIS CATEGORIES**

Teacher talk

1	Accepts and clarifies the feelings of the students in a non-threatening way.
2	Praises or encourages students.
3	Accepts or uses ideas of students.
4	Asks questions for students to answer.
5	Lectures.
6	Gives directions.
7	Criticises students or justifies own authority.

Students' talk

8	Students talk in response to teacher.
9	Talk by students which they initiate.
10	Silence or confusion.

The observer writes down every three seconds the category which best describes what is taking place in the classroom. It is best used in what might be called 'formal' lessons.

(Wragg, E.C. & Kerry, T.L., *Rediguide 14: Classroom Interaction Research*, University of Nottingham School of Education, 1982)

ITEM C USING STRUCTURED OBSERVATION

In a small proportion of the lessons I observed I made use of the Flanders Interaction Analysis Categories. A mark is made on the grid, in the appropriate category, at frequent and regular intervals during the process of a lesson to record the communication events just completed. Even in this small sample of 24 lessons, a clear difference between bands emerged in the proportion of the teachers' time spent in 'criticizing or justifying authority'.

(Stephen Ball, *Beachside Comprehensive*, Cambridge University Press, 1981)

ITEM D THE POLITICS OF RESEARCH FINDINGS

Sociologists have continually pretended that it (Sociology) can come up with the goods necessary to change this or that problem. It has disappointed because it remains part of an intellectual workforce that is in some sense apart from the society that it is investigating. As a consequence it has never had the real contacts with social and political forces to give any weight to the elements of change that are contained in its work. It has investigated, published and, to a large extent, sat back waiting; nothing has happened so it has started another investigation...

In this work I think I have identified a large group of people in society (working class youth) that sees itself as being pushed around in a way that is sometimes very humiliating and always quite confusing. I have identified that this group does not have either the consciousness or the political power to get out of this situation on its own. I have also identified political struggle on a much wider level as being the only overall solution... What is important, then, is the nature of the political struggle that can be carried out to change the situation.

(Paul Corrigan, *Schooling the Smash Street Kids*, Macmillan, London, 1979)

a) What does Pat McNeill mean in Item A when he asks the sociologist if his account is 'valid'? (2 marks)

b) In what ways does the researcher in Item A attempt to improve the validity of this research? (4 marks)

c) What are the advantages of using Flanders Interaction Analysis Categories (FIAC) over more unstructured methods? (5 marks)

d) What are the disadvantages of using FIAC? (4 marks)

e) Assess the view expressed by Paul Corrigan that sociology should not be value-free but that sociologists should side with working class youth in political struggle. (10 marks)

Question 2 **Research Techniques and the Family**

ITEM A RESEARCH INTO THE EFFECTS OF UNEMPLOYMENT

We approached the Department of Health and Social Security who were planning a nationwide study of the unemployed. We asked the DHSS whether we could interview approximately twenty two-parent families as far as possible with dependent children, where the male breadwinner had been unemployed for at least sixteen weeks and had been employed throughout the previous year. The reason for this timing was because we had to interview them after the DHSS had seen them for the second time, sixteen to twenty-four weeks after the men had registered, and then select our sample from their computerised results. We were therefore looking at a sample who had spent a longer time than average out of work, and who would probably have more difficulties in returning to it.

132 families fell into our criteria. A letter was sent by the DHSS to these families asking them whether they would volunteer to participate in our project. 72 families replied saying they did not want to participate, leaving us with 60, or 45.5% of our original sample.

(Leonard Fagin and Martin Little, *The Forsaken Families*, Penguin, Harmondsworth, 1984)

ITEM B RESEARCHING PATTERNS OF INFANT CARE

Social survey interviewers need to have a pleasant manner and a certain skill in persuading cooperation. Our interviewing programme also demanded special skills related to the particular subject we were investigating. It was clear at the outset that we could use only women interviewers; but they also needed to be reasonably mature and intelligent people, able to discuss the intimate details of birth and child rearing without causing the mothers too much embarrassment. After all, it may not be easy to discuss such matters as breast feeding and toilet training with someone you have only just met.

A full-scale project only really became possible when the City Health Department offered to let their health visitors undertake a large proportion of the interviews... they already had access to the very homes in which we were interested, and they had generally been visiting the mother regularly since the baby was two weeks old.

UNIVERSITY OF NOTTINGHAM
CHILD HEALTH RESEARCH UNIT

Clinic District ....
Interviewer ....
Date ....

GUIDED INTERVIEW SCHEDULE
(*for mothers of children aged* 1:0)

Breast feeding
If little or no breast feeding: Did you have any special reason for not breast feeding? ....

If any breast feeding: Did you enjoy feeding the baby? ....
....

Does he ever have temper tantrums? Frequently/sometimes/never
What seems to start them off? ....
....
What do you do? ....
....
How do you punish him when he's been naughty? (*mother's own words*) ....
....

Sleep pattern during previous day and night
What time was he put to bed last night? ....
How soon after that did he go to sleep? ....
Did he wake during the night? YES/NO
If YES: at what time(s)? ....
How long did he stay awake? ....

Does he play with his body much? (Prompt) Playing with nose/scratching face/pulling hair/pulling eyelashes/playing with toes/sucking fingers, etc./playing with the private parts/head-banging
....
If other than sucking: Do you try to stop him at all? YES/NO

(John and Elizabeth Newson, *Patterns of Infant Care*, Penguin, Harmondsworth, 1963)

Can you remember what actually led up to the first time he hit you then? I mean, as you say, it was...

It's only now that I remember back. It's just that we used to sit and quarrel and he'd end up going for me. I don't know. I used to feel that he was very jealous and I couldn't wear make-up or anything if I got all dressed up and that. That's how the arguments used to start. I hadn't even sort of gone out, but I'd maybe feel like doing myself up. He'd start hitting me, you know.

And can you remember what happened that first time? How he hit you? Was it just a punch?

He just punched me under the chin actually. I seen stars.

Was it just the once the first time?

Uh-huh.

Did you hit him back?

I was too astounded. I'd never been hit before, so I was just standing there for the short time that I had to take it.

And can you recall what time of day that was?

It was always, nearly always, night time.

And did it happen in your house?

Well, at the time, yes, it was a house.

Can you recall, was it the living room, or the kitchen, or the bedroom?

It was in the living room.

(R. Emerson Dobash and Russell Dobash, *Violence Against Wives*, Open Books, Shepton Mallet, 1980)

---

a) How representative is the sample in Item A? (4 marks)

b) Explain the advantages and disadvantages of using female health visitors to research patterns of infant care in Item B. (6 marks)

c) What criticisms could be made of the interview schedule in Item B? (2 marks)

d) With reference to Item C assess the usefulness of the unstructured interview in sociological research. (6 marks)

e) Which of the data here would be most likely to influence social policy and why? (7 marks)

Question 3 **Sociology and Race**

ITEM A **THE IMMIGRANT-HOST MODEL**

Consensus theory lays emphasis on immigrant status. An implicit assumption of the theory was a picture of the host society as characterised by a fundamental agreement on basic values. Since cultural consensus is deemed necessary, the chief onus is on the immigrants themselves to change. This will allow cultural differences to be minimised and will result in assimilation.

This host-immigrant framework was developed in the United States to account for the assimilation of immigrants into American society. Although the process was not a smooth one, entailing to begin with reliance on an ethnic community as a source of identification and protection, over time individuals were able to enter the wider society and gain mobility within it.

Park generalised from the American experience to argue that, 'in the relations of races there is a cycle of events which tends everywhere to repeat itself . . . (and) . . . which takes the form of contacts, competition, accommodation and eventual assimilation and is apparently progressive and irreversible.'

(Andrew Pilkington, *Race Relations in Britain*, UTP, Slough, 1984)

ITEM B RESEARCHING RACIAL DISCRIMINATION

The television series Black and White explored the extent of racism in the city of Bristol. The research was carried out by two journalists – one black, Geoff Small, the other white, Tim Marshall. They chose Bristol because its percentage of blacks (4%) is the same as that for the British population as a whole.

Small and Marshall researched racism in areas where discrimination is illegal: housing, employment, and places of entertainment (such as night clubs and discos). Typically, their approach was for Geoff Small, the black journalist, to apply for the job, or whatever, first, and for Tim Marshall to apply later. They took care to check that the service was still available when Marshall applied.

These are some of their main findings. Five out of 15 bed-and-breakfast proprietors discriminated. Three out of 16 landlords/ladies of rented accommodation discriminated. Four out of ten employers discriminated when applications were made in person. Two out of eight night-clubs discriminated.

One reviewer of the series regretted that viewers only saw the cases in which discrimination occurred and not 'how sane, unbigoted, at-ease people commonly deal with the issue.'

This is a fair observation but it misses the point from a black person's perspective. The point – as Small says several times – is that a black person can never be sure when she/he is being treated equally as a person or being discriminated against on grounds of colour.

(Mike O'Donnell, 'Racial Discrimination', *New Society*, 27 May 1988)

ITEM C DISCRIMINATION IN NOTTINGHAM

Three test candidates applied by letter for advertised job vacancies, one a native white person; the other two were black, of West Indian and Asian origins. Each applicant was equally matched in terms of qualifications, previous job experience, age and sex. Three standard letters of application were used which enabled the content, structure and style of letter and hand-writing ability of the test applicants to be strictly controlled and equally matched.

The only variable factor in the tests was the ethnic origin of the applicants.

JUNIOR CLERK VACANCY FOR ACCOUNTS DEPARTMENT OF A MAJOR FURNITURE MANUFACTURER

Letter of application from West Indian tester, 3 August 1977

Dear Madam,

I should like to apply for the vacancy of Clerk which you advertised in todays Evening Post.

I am aged 18½ years old and came from Jamaica to Nottingham in 1965. I left school in summer 1975 with C.S.E. Physics and Chemistry Grade 1, French Grade 2, and Woodwork Grade 2; also G.C.E. 'O' level in English Literature Grade C and Mathematics Grade B. I also have C.S.E. Grade 1 in English, Maths and Art. Since leaving school I have been working in a building contractors offices in the City doing general work including accounting.

I should be pleased to come for an interview at any time suitable to you.

Yours faithfully,
Leroy Grant

Letter of application from the white tester, 3 August 1977

Dear Madam,

I should like to apply for the position of Clerk as advertised in todays Evening Post.

I left school in May 1975 and worked in a large factory in Leicester doing general costing and stock control work. I left this job in June 1977 when my parents moved back to Nottingham to settle.

At school I got G.C.E. 'O' level Geography (D), Mathematics (B), English (C) and C.S.E. in Technical Drawing (1), Engineering (2) and Physical Science (3).

I am available to attend for interview at any time convenient to you.

Yours sincerely,
Stephen Kirk

Employer's reply to West Indian tester, 17 August 1977

Dear Mr. Grant,

We thank you for your letter in reply to our advertisement for an Accounts Clerk.

We had a great response to the advertisement so regret that it was impossible to interview all applicants. The post has now been filled.

We should like to thank you for the interest you have shown in the Company and wish you success in finding a suitable position in the not too distant future.

Yours sincerely,

Personnel Officer

Reply to the white tester, 12 August 1977

Dear Mr. Kirk,

We thank you for your application in reply to our advertisement for an Accounts Clerk.

Could you please attend an interview on Monday next, August 15th at 11.45 a.m.

Should either the date or the time prove inconvenient to you please give me a ring (phone number given) and I will endeavour to arrange an alternative appointment.

Yours sincerely,

Personnel Officer

The reply to Asian tester on 17 August 19787 was the same as for the West Indian tester.

(Jim Hubbuck and Simon Carter, *Half a Chance?* Commission for Racial Equality, London, 1980)

ITEM D OTHER SOURCES OF DATA

Very limited use was made of data published in books, of parliamentary papers and monographs, to orient the study historically and in particular to demonstrate that West Indians face a double problem of poverty and identity-confusion due to imperialism, and that their slave heritage was of paramount importance in determining the variations in their reactions to discrimination in Britain.

In addition, quite a lot of factual information was gleaned from back-dated copies of the Bristol Evening Post and official documents published by the Bristol city corporation. To fill in gaps in the data gathered through pure observation, as well as to augment the biographical details of some of my informants it was necessary also to pay several visits to the offices of local probation officers, who allowed me access to their files.

(Ken Pryce, *Endless Pressure*, Penguin, Harmondsworth, 1979)

a) Which sociological perspective is the Immigrant-Host Model associated with? Illustrate your answer with reference to Item A. (4 marks)

b) What term is used to describe the type of data gathered by Ken Pryce in Item D and what are the advantages of this kind of data? (3 marks)

c) Why are sociological experiments, mentioned in Items B and C, often used in research into racial discrimination? (4 marks)

d) What criticisms could be made of the evidence produced by the experiments, described in Items B and C, and why are experiments so rarely used in other sociological research? (7 marks)

e) What factors might influence sociologists in their choice of ethnic minorities as an area to study? (7 marks)

Question 4 **Interactionist Research**

ITEM A **DEFINING THE SITUATION**

The Symbolic Interactionist disbars himself from making external judgements about the people he studies. Instead he must get close to them and describe their circumstances as they see them. He adopts the position of describing the competing and conflicting claims men make about what is 'real' and 'what is happening'. He does not seek to arbitrate between these claims, to say which ones are correct.

(E.C. Cuff and G.C.F. Payne, *Perspectives in Sociology*, 2nd edition, Unwin Hyman, London, 1984)

ITEM B **RESEARCH IN AN ASYLUM**

My immediate object in doing field work at St. Elizabeth's Hospital was to try to learn about the social world of the hospital inmate, as this world is subjectively experienced by him. I started out in the role of an assistant to the athletic director... and I passed the day with patients, avoiding sociable contact with the staff and the carrying of a key. I did not sleep in the wards, and the top hospital management knew what my aims were.

It was then and still is my belief that any group of persons – prisoners, primitives, pilots, or patients – develop a life of their own that becomes meaningful, reasonable, and normal once you get close to it, and a good way to learn about any of these worlds is to submit oneself in the company of the members to the daily round of (events) to which they are subject.

To describe the patient's situation faithfully is necessarily to present a partisan view. For this bias I partly excuse myself by arguing that the imbalance is at least on the right side of the scale, since almost all professional literature on mental patients is written from the point of view of the psychiatrist.

(Erving Goffman, *Asylums*, Penguin, Harmondsworth, 1961)

ITEM C **PROBLEMS OF RESEARCHING A RELIGIOUS SECT**

Why should – how could – anyone become a Moonie? What possible explanation is there for the fact that men and women will sacrifice their family, their friends and their careers in order to sell tracts (books), flowers or candy on the streets for sixteen, eighteen or even twenty hours a day?

It was obvious that no one method would be sufficient to obtain all the information that I would need for such a venture. I would need to speak to outsiders as well as insiders. I needed information about individual Moonies, their backgrounds, their hopes, values and general perspectives on life both inside and outside the movement. I also needed to observe them 'at work' as they interacted with other people in order to see how they were influenced by, and would themselves influence, others on a day-to-day basis.

I decided that three main approaches were needed: in-depth interviews, participant observation and questionnaires.

I believe that it is perfectly possible to learn to see things from other people's point of view without necessarily agreeing that they are right. At the same time it seems to be self-evidently true that, whatever judgements we make, they will be 'better' judgements to the extent that they are based on an accurate understanding of whatever it is we are judging.

There are, however, those who think that it is immoral for the sociologist to sit on the fence. Both Moonies and their adversaries have complained bitterly about certain of my articles in which I have not come down on one side or the other. .... When I challenged a clergyman, who had told some parents that I was unreliable, to tell me what it was that I had got wrong, he replied, 'Oh, you get the facts right, but it's no good if you don't come out strongly and clearly against them (the Moonies) – people will be lulled into thinking everything's all right'.

(Eileen Barker, *The Making of a Moonie*, Basil Blackwell, Oxford, 1984)

a) What methods do Symbolic Interactionist researchers use to 'get close' to people and so be able to 'describe their circumstances as they see them' (Item A)? (2 marks)

b) What method did Goffman use to do this research in Item B and what are its advantages? (4 marks)

c) What methods were used by Eileen Barker in Item C and why? (6 marks)

d) In the light of Eileen Barker's experience, what problems might sociologists face when they try to describe society 'from other people's point of view'? (5 marks)

e) Can and should sociology be value-free? Illustrate your answer using Items A-C and from elsewhere if you wish. (8 marks)

Question 5 **Researching Education**

ITEM A **RESEARCH IN A COMPREHENSIVE SCHOOL**

I began my work at Beachside Comprehensive in the Autumn Term of 1973, starting with a period of general observation and familiarization. My aim was 'to locate a number of strategic areas that would enable me to gain a clear picture of the processes taking place within the school'.

My participation in the daily life of the school, apart from observing of lessons, etc., was by supply-teaching... plus four periods of timetable teaching... I also accompanied forms on school visits, went on one school trip, invigilated in exams, took registers for absent teachers, played in the staff v. pupils cricket match, and so on.

I observed a large number of lessons but I also interviewed pupils and teachers, carried out several small-scale questionnaire studies, sociometric and otherwise, and worked through and analysed school records and registers.

The teachers' own descriptions of the early behaviour of 2TA show that the form did not appear initially to conform to the stereotypes applied to them,

'They were delightful, for the first six months they were one of the forms that everyone talked about as being lively and enthusiastic. Then the rot set in and they began to assert themselves as individuals and they began to lose their form identity.' (Form Teacher)

Some measure of the beginnings of anti-school behaviour by members of the form can be gained from remarks in their personal files:

'stealing from shops'
'rude to staff, mother asked to visit school'
'cheeky and unco-operative in lessons'
'nuisance in assembly'

Some of the pupils in 2TA were now very frequently 'in trouble', both informally in face to face conflict with teachers and formally in detention. Here is a typical classroom incident.

Second year Maths (setted group), lesson notes:
The group contains eleven pupils from 2TA. There is a lot of talking; the teacher issues a continuous stream of individual rebukes.
Teacher: 'When we do something together you've got to listen.'
She is explaining how to do multiplication with a slide rule. Corina is turned completely round talking to the girls behind her. The teacher stops and waits.
Teacher: 'We are waiting for the same old people'...

A further illustration of the progressive change in the school behaviour of the band 2 pupils, and the emergence of differences between them and the band 1 pupils, is their record of attendance over the first and second years:

Case-study forms: average number of sessions absent per pupil in each term

	Term 1	Term 2	Term 3
ICU	7.53	9.45	8.10
1TA	6.66	7.70	9.47
	Term 4	Term 5	Term 5
2CU	8.13	11.64	9.15
2TA	12.59	13.22	12.64

(Adapted from Stephen Ball, *Beachside Comprehensive*, Cambridge University Press, Cambridge, 1981)

ITEM B A SURVEY OF SCHOOL CHILDREN

This study of children in the primary school years is the third main report on a follow-up investigation which began in 1945 and was originally undertaken to examine the availability and effectiveness of the ante-natal and maternity service in Britain.

It had not originally been intended to research beyond the 1946 study. But the potential value of a follow-up study was so evident, that a superb opportunity would have been missed if some institution had not attempted to keep in touch with the children and their families, recording their experience in respect of problems of health and growth, of educational development and social change.

The children in this survey are drawn from every type of family and every part of the country. Their parents include at one extreme eminent artists, scientists and politicians and, at the other, unemployed labourers. They are scattered all over Great Britain from the Scilly Isles to the Shetlands.

All the 5,362 children have one thing in common: they were born during the first week of March 1946. Illegitimate children and twins were excluded, but apart from this all children born during this week to the wives of non-manual workers and of farm labourers, and one-quarter of those born to the wives of other types of manual workers and self-employed persons are included.

The greater part of the educational information used in this study was provided by the primary and preparatory school teachers, who kept special records of school absences and the reasons for them, and reported at intervals on the behaviour of the children and on their attitudes to work. They also supervised the giving of a series of tests of mental ability and school achievement, when the children were 8 years old and again, when they were 11.

(Adapted from J.W.B. Douglas, *The Home and the School*, Panther Books, London, 1964)

ITEM C **TALKING TO 'THE LADS'**

There follows an edited transcription of a group discussion recorded in January 1977 at the University, with some of 'the lads' from the Hammertown School who had read early drafts of the book. The discussion centred on how my role as a researcher had been seen and what the 'results' of the research meant to them.

Spanksy It was nice to be out of lessons (note: for group discussions).

Perc Oh yeah, that was about it wor it, nice to be out of lessons.

Joey ...I thought, you know, I thought he's not doin' this for his own sake, he's doin' it 'cos, y'know, somebody's put 'im up to it and he wants to find out why we do it, y'know, do a 1987 (note: refers to Orwell's *1984*) thing and cut parts of yer brain out and...You were virtually the answer to our prayer, because, do you remember, we used to make vague attempts at writing accounts of things we'd done at school...

Bill ...I thought, y'know, we'll have to kinda watch out for this, y'know. He's gonna let Peters (Headmaster) and all them lot know what's goin' on, and then after a bit y'know, I realised that wasn't right and that I just enjoyed it 'cos it was a skive...

Perc ...I used to think you were asking a bit much, personal things y'know.

Paul Willis Do you mean in the group discussions or the individual ones?

Perc Individual, I'd y'know, I doe mind talkin' to yer on me own, I'd, y'know...when yer with yer mates yer say a lot of things yer know that don't really happen...

(Paul Willis, *Learning to Labour*, Gower, Farnborough, 1977)

a) What research methods were used by Stephen Ball in Item A? (2 marks)

b) Item A is an extract from a case study of one comprehensive school. Assess the usefulness of this technique for our understanding of the education system. (6 marks)

c) Evaluate Douglas's use of teachers to gather data in Item B. (4 marks)

d) Identify the research method used by Willis in Item C. What advantages and disadvantages of the method are suggested in Item C? (6 marks)

e) With reference to sociological theory and methods, compare the approach of Douglas and Ball. (7 marks)

Question 6 **Sociological Research and the Media**

ITEM A THE GLASGOW UNIVERSITY MEDIA GROUP

The Glasgow Media Group has established itself as one of the leading groups of researchers on the mass media, and its critical view of television news broadcasting has meant that it has come under frequent attack from within the BBC and ITV companies. Its research has become embroiled in contentious political disputes. The group was formed in 1974 with the intention of monitoring the broadcasting of industrial news, and it rapidly became a semi-permanent research unit within the Sociology Department at Glasgow University.

The Group's research relies heavily on video recordings, using the methods of content analysis. Its initial objective was to disclose the picture of industrial relations presented in news broadcasts. Official statistics on employment and strikes were used as points of comparison for the 'facts' presented in the news. The Group was particularly interested in the language used in industrial reporting: it was concerned with the ways in which particular words convey images and stereotypes which interlock to form a specific world view. The use of words such as 'dispute', 'militant', 'threat', 'trouble', and 'demands', conveys the idea that workers are responsible for conflict between the two 'sides' of industry, and the Glasgow University Media Group claims that this reflects a systematic bias in favour of government and the employers.

('Research roundup', *Social Studies Review*, Vol.2, No.1, September 1986)

ITEM B THE MEDIA AND WOMEN PEACE PROTESTORS

We analysed the coverage of six women's peace demonstrations that appeared on the news between December 1982 and December 1983, in a total of 38 bulletins; and compared it with other reports including some from the women who participated. We found that many features central to the camp (Greenham Common) were not covered in the news... what exactly is the political protest the camp is making? The broadcasters have grasped the fundamental idea that the camp is opposed to Cruise missiles – although even this is not always made clear. Coverage on the two ITV evening bulletins and BBC 2's *Newsnight* of the opening of the five-day blockade at Greenham Common avoided giving any reason at all for the women's action.

The news does not give any publicity to the women's case. Opposition to Cruise is mentioned, and some 'anti-nuclear message' is referred to, but the women have no chance to explain exactly why they oppose Cruise, why they are anti-nuclear... Of course 'putting across the anti-nuclear message' is not the broadcaster's job; but they are falling down on the job of providing informative reporting if they cover the demonstrations without explaining (or allowing the demonstrators to explain) what they are trying to say.

(Glasgow University Media Group, *War and Peace News*, Open University Press, Milton Keynes, 1985)

ITEM C A MEDIA MAN'S REPLY

Alongside the need to provide high quality material and a critical base against which to judge it, broadcasters must engage actively with educators and others in the debate about TV and radio and their role in society, providing accurate and comprehensive information on all aspects of the subject from the standpoint of the practitioners. They may do this through writing, through speaking, by discussions, and through encouraging research, but if they do not do these things then they leave the field wide open to tendentious (one-sided), ideologically simplistic arguments which are bad scholarship and a disservice to real education.

The work of the Glasgow Media Group which seems to inform some media studies is a case in point. One does not object to polemic (controversial discussions), especially if it appears to make some telling points, but polemic dressed as academic research is more difficult to take. The tone of the volumes so far produced is biased and arrogant, the very qualities being attributed to the broadcasters. Yet this very work is being quoted endlessly as if it had some 'scientific' validity.

(John Cain, 'A role for broadcasters', 1985, in Manuel Alvarado et al, *Learning the Media*, Macmillan, Basingstoke, 1987)

ITEM D ATTITUDES TO TV NEWS

Q. Now I am going to mention some things people sometimes say about TV news programmes. Please tell me whether you tend to agree or disagree with each.

	Agree	Disagree	Don't know
TV news stories about violence have made Britons more fearful than they were in the days before there was television	79	15	6
TV news stories should run more stories about good news and fewer stories about violence	65	27	8
TV news is just as interested in exploring the causes of violence as it is in reporting violent acts	58	30	12
TV news runs lots of crime stories because that's what people are interested in hearing about	47	45	9

Note: Gallup interviewers have strict quotas which means that they must obtain, in a sample of ten people, a required number of men and women of different age groups, of different social classes and in employment or otherwise. Sample size is approximately 1,000 adults.

(Gordon Heald and Robert J.Wybrow, *The Gallup Survey of Britain*, Croom Helm, Beckenham, 1986)

a) The research method used by the Glasgow University Media Group (GUMG) in Item A is called content analysis. What are the advantages and disadvantages of this method? (4 marks)

b) Suggest two other research topics apart from television news which could be researched in this way. (2 marks)

c) Assess the data in Item D referring to its validity, reliability and representativeness. (4 marks)

d) The broadcaster in Item C accuses the GUMG of being biased. Explain and assess this view illustrating your answers with evidence from Items A and B. (5 marks)

e) In Item C the broadcaster accuses the GUMG research of lacking 'scientific validity'. What do you think he means by 'science'? How might the Glasgow researchers answer this criticism? (10 marks)

Question 7 **Researching Deviance**

ITEM A **MORAL PANICS**

The sociology of moral panics has enjoyed a high profile within the analysis of social problems ever since Stan Cohen coined the term in 1972 within his study of the 'mods and rockers' phenomenon of the mid-sixties. In the past two decades the concept of 'moral panic' has been used to describe official reactions to, or perhaps more pertinently media reactions to, mugging, soccer violence, social security 'scroungers', child abuse, vandalism, drug use, student militancy, 'spectacular' youth subcultures, street crime, permissiveness and indeed crime and deviance in general.

Moral panic is a much used catch-all phrase to refer to a public fear of crime, deviance and disorder; it implies that such fear is exaggerated and out of proportion to the real threat offered.

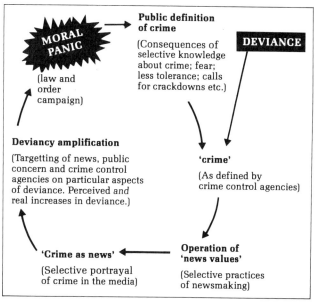

(John Muncie, 'Much ado about nothing? The sociology of moral panics', *Social Studies Review*, Vol.3, No.2, November 1987)

ITEM B THE BRITISH CRIME SURVEY

Pat McNeill: The British Crime Survey was set up in 1982 to investigate crime through a sample survey which asks people about their experience of crime. What prompted its establishment?

Pat Mayhew (Principal Research Officer at the Home Office Research and Planning Unit): It is recognised that the official statistics of crime have their limitations. There were already established victim surveys in the USA (since 1972), in Canada, and in Australia. There was growing concern about crime, and the Summer of 1981 was that of the riots. There was a need for more information, and victim surveys give a more rounded picture than police statistics. BCSs have been published in 1983 and 1985 and the third will appear in 1989. The more surveys you do, the more useful the data becomes, because it is then possible to analyse trends. This is valuable data for the Home Office, which funds the research.

PMcN: What is the design of the survey?

PM: Many forms of crime are rare, so we have to have a big sample, about 11,000 households. In 1982 the only feasible sampling frame was the electoral register. Today, PAF (Post Office Address File) is a better frame and in 1988 we thought about whether to switch to it. But we found that this might mean a loss of comparability.

PMcN: Are you aware of any particular weak areas in the data?

PM: Yes, the measurement of domestic abuse and of sexual assault...

(Pat McNeill, 'A chronicle of crime', *New Statesman and Society*, 9 December 1988)

ITEM C THE ISLINGTON CRIME SURVEY

Studies like the Home Office's well-known British Crime Survey have revolutionised thinking about crime. By asking people direct about the crimes they have experienced, such studies give us a much more reliable measure of the extent of crime. In particular, they allow us to chart the 'dark figure' of crime previously unknown—about half of which turns out to be serious crime... the London borough of Islington last year commissioned the Centre for Criminology at Middlesex Polytechnic to conduct a survey of the extent of crime in the area, and to assess the public's evaluation of police performance. A random sample of 2,000 households were surveyed.

It is sometimes suggested that crime, although frequent, is a minor irritant, given the range of problems the city dweller has to contend with. The public, on this view, suffer from hysteria about crime. Panics abound—particularly about mugging, sexual assault and violence—which are out of touch with reality.

But the inner city dweller is not the average citizen. Our study, with its ability to focus in on the highly victimised, indicates the realism of their fears.

It is scarcely odd that 46 per cent of people in Islington should admit to worrying 'a lot' about mugging, given that over 40 per cent of the borough's population actually know someone (including themselves and their family), who has been mugged in the last twelve months. Nor is it unrealistic to worry about burglary when its incidence in the borough runs at five times the national average.

Why are women more fearful about crime than men, when most studies show they have a far less chance of becoming victims? Our survey suggests that, in the inner city at least, their fears are perfectly rational. Women here are more likely to be victims of crime than men.

The reason for the shortfall in past findings is the nature of many of the crimes committed against women, and their reluctance to admit them to a stranger engaged in a social survey. Using carefully trained, sympathetic researchers, we found a considerably higher rate for female victims. The reason is threefold: sexual assaults are almost exclusively a female 'prerogative'; so is domestic violence; and street robbery against women is greater than it is against men.

(Trevor Jones and Jock Young, 'Crime, police and people', *New Society*, 24 January 1986)

a) Which sociological perspective is suggested by the concept of a 'moral panic'? Support your answer by using the data in Item A. (4 marks)

b) With reference to Item B explain how sociologists choose a sample, the problems they may encounter choosing a sample and why sample choice is important. (6 marks)

c) Both Items B and C refer to the problems of validity and reliability in researching crimes against women. What are these problems and how do sociologists try to overcome them? (6 marks)

d) Referring to the data, explain the advantages and disadvantages of positivist and interpretivist (or phenomenological) approaches to the study of deviance. (9 marks)

Question 8 **Personal Documents**

ITEM A **RESEARCH DIARIES**

The 'home-centredness' of the pupils noted in the second year was less evident in the third. The number of unsupervised activities with their peers increased, and their social horizons also broadened, both in terms of types of activities, references to 'pop-concerts', etc., and in terms of time spent away from Beachside itself. Wallsea (the nearest seaside town) was now commonly mentioned in the diaries pupils kept for me...

John Dyson's Diary
1 May. Went to Dursiton (small town nearby) Sports Centre and played squash.
2 May. In the afternoon I went to the pictures in Wallsea to see 'The Man with the Golden Gun' with Simon.
7 May. In the afternoon I went into Wallsea with Simon. We went on the pier and I won 30p, then we saw 'Blazing Saddles' and 'Now for Something Completely Different'.
8 May. At 8pm I went to Graham Starker's party (a boy in another Band 1 class) with Rich and Simon and got home about 11pm slightly drunk!

For most band 1 pupils, schoolwork continued to impinge considerably upon their out-of-school time in the form of homework and revision for exams.

Kathleen Hopkins's Diary
10 February. Cathy phoned and came round at 7.30 we played my new L.P. and tried to revise.

For the anti-school Band 2 pupils and some Band 1 pupils, the influence of school is less pervasive, and they attach less importance to it. There are no mentions of revising for exams in the diary entries recorded by Band 2 pupils.

Belinda Hammett's Diary

16 February. I went to see my Gran in the morning and in the afternoon I watched telly. At six o'clock I listened to the Top 20 on the radio in the bath. Then I watched the film on television and went to bed.

17 February. At school we had our exams, first we had Music and then French and Physics, we had a Maths lesson but we've got the exam tomorrow. Daphne came around in the evening to listen to my records.

(Stephen Ball, *Beachside Comprehensive*, Cambridge University Press, Cambridge, 1981)

ITEM B MASS-OBSERVATION DAY-SURVEY MARCH 12, 1937

(Note: Mass Observation began in 1937. It involved several hundred volunteers writing factual diaries of their experiences on the 12th day of each month.)

5pm. Arrive home. Leave parcels in hall and call at next door neighbour's to see if laundry has been left there. Notice on small piece of paper on neighbour's step says 'please leave grocery at back door.' Knock door. Neighbour comes to door with eye-glasses in her hand. Gives me laundry. Says 'I can't keep the door open in case the cat gets out. There's the greengrocer at the back-door.'

Back in own house. Take off M.'s outdoor clothes and own. Give M. the snow-plough and crayons. Put the bear on the mantelpiece with camel and hippopotamus. Look through *Holiday Haunts*.

5.25. Go out into kitchen to prepare tea. Lay tea, cut bread and butter, etc.

5.40. H. arrives. Gives me the *Daily Telegraph* and *New Statesman*, but has forgotten to bring me in the local paper. I give him the shrub and he goes out and plants it. Greengrocer comes to the door. I show him some rotten apples he gave me last time he called. He says he will replace them. I order eggs, cauliflower, cabbage, onions, apples, lettuce and watercress. Go into kitchen and make tea.

6.00. Call in H. from garden. We have tea.

6.45. I read to M.

7.15. Take M. up and put him to bed.

7.30. Come downstairs and wash up crockery.

7.55. Typing...

(Humphrey Jennings and Charles Madge (editors), *Mass-Observation Day-Survey May 12 1937*, Faber and Faber, London, 1987)

ITEM C A CRIMINAL'S DEFENCE

I have already served ten years in prison and even on an optimistic count I must serve another ten years of my current sentence before I can realistically hope to be paroled. No one can waste so much of the past and forfeit so much of the future as I have without thinking deeply about the reasons for his behaviour. I know what has happened in my life and I think I know the reasons for it.

I was bolder than most of the others in annoying and playing up the teachers. This was not because I was disturbed in my life at home. Rather, it was because I sought prestige by overconforming to the standards of behaviour of the peer group I identified with, in compensation for my lack of acceptable parental approval.

I had not become a thief and a thug for the material rewards. Money, of course, provides a goal and a rationalization for much crime, but it also provides a cover for the motives and drives of the criminal. I became committed to a criminal code before I was engaged in criminal acts.

(John McVicar, *McVicar by Himself*, Hutchinson, London, 1974)

ITEM D A CRIMINAL'S DEFENCE REASSESSED

...the book with all its accounts of childhood and causes was written originally as my defence statement, when I'd been picked up again after the escape. It was really written for people like probation officers.

(John McVicar, quoted in Laurie Taylor, *In the Underworld*, Unwin, London, 1984)

a) Using sociological concepts, assess the value of the research diary illustrated in Item A.   (6 marks)

b) Suggest another topic where research diaries would produce useful data. Give reasons for your answer.   (3 marks)

c) What are the advantages of Mass-Observation (Item B) over unstructured interviews?   (4 marks)

d) Using Items C and D assess the value of John McVicar's analysis of his past.   (5 marks)

e) Personal documents often present practical problems for researchers. Explain what these are, referring to collection and analysis, and suggest how they might be overcome.   (7 marks)

Question 9 **Values and Sociology**

ITEM A **SPEAKING FOR THE UNDERDOG**

Whose viewpoint shall we present? There are two considerations here, one practical and the other moral. The practical consideration is that the viewpoint of conventional society toward deviance is usually well known. Therefore, we ought to study the views of those who participate in deviant activities, because in this way we will fill out the most obscure part of the picture.

It is in the nature of deviance that it will be difficult for anyone to study both sides of the process and accurately capture the perspectives of both classes of participants, rule-breakers and rule enforcers. Not that it is impossible, but practical considerations of gaining access to situations and the confidence of the people involved in any reasonable length of time mean that one will probably study the situation from one side or the other. Whichever class of participants we choose to study and whose viewpoint we therefore choose to take, we will probably be accused of 'bias'.

(Adapted from Howard S. Becker, *Outsiders*, Free Press, New York, 1963)

ITEM B CRITICAL SOCIOLOGY

I want to defend the view that sociology, understood in the manner in which I shall describe it, necessarily has a subversive quality. Its subversive or critical character, however, I shall argue, does not carry with it (or should not do so) the implication that it is an intellectually disreputable enterprise. On the contrary, it is exactly because sociology deals with problems which are the objects of major controversies and conflicts in society itself, that it has this character... the study of sociology, appropriately understood, unavoidably demonstrates how fundamental are the social questions that have to be faced in today's world. Everyone is to some extent aware of these questions, but the study of sociology helps bring them into much sharper focus. Sociology cannot remain a purely academic subject, if 'academic' means a disinterested and remotely scholarly pursuit, followed within the enclosed walls of the university.

(Anthony Giddens, *Sociology: A Brief but Critical Introduction*, 2nd Ed Macmillan, Basingstoke, 1986)

ITEM C SOCIOLOGY AND LEFT-WING BIAS

Yesterday David Marsland a leading sociologist published a devastating indictment of his own profession. Here he explains why the teaching of sociology is a deeply destructive force in Britain today.

Sociology is the enemy within. It is an enemy that sows the seeds of bankruptcy and influences huge numbers of impressionable people with a bias I wish to expose.

Such words are, I know, a serious condemnation of a whole profession. But for some time now I have looked at the attitudes displayed by sociologists – I am one myself.

And if, as my own evidence shows, sociologists are neglecting their responsibility for accurate, objective description and biasing their analyses of contemporary Britain to an enormous extent, something has to be done urgently.

As the teaching of history has declined in this country, sociology increasingly provides young people's main entree to an understanding of the nature and prospects of their own society.

This would be fine were it not for the fact that huge numbers of students are being influenced by the biased one-sidedness of contemporary sociology.

(*Daily Mail*, 31 March 1988)

ITEM D THE RIVINGTON LECTURE: RT HON KENNETH BAKER MP

Social scientists have so eagerly (put forward) excuses for the inexcusable. Concepts of right and wrong behaviour became blurred by justifications of behaviour and acts which should have been regarded by any civilised society as unacceptable at any time. Social scientists tended to argue that behavioural patterns were only the products of social, political and economic factors. Vandalism, hooliganism and crimes of violence were all to be seen simply as part and parcel of an increasingly affluent, materialistic, secular and normless society.

(Kenneth Baker, 8 November 1988)

Perhaps the most serious problem with Professor Marsland's position is that he slips from advocating an 'unbiased' approach to asserting that sociology should be 'positive' about existing social arrangements. It is not the business of any scientific discipline to make 'positive' or 'negative' judgements. The job of social science is to describe, analyse and explain, not to evaluate. Professor Marsland completely misunderstands this simple point and seeks to incorporate his own political preferences into sociological research.

(British Sociological Association, *Press Release*, March 30 1988)

a) How would Becker (Item A) answer the accusation that his sociology of deviance is biased? (3 marks)

b) According to Giddens in Item B, sociology deals with problems 'which are the objects of major controversies and conflicts in society...' What does this mean and why does this often result in sociology being seen as subversive? (5 marks)

c) What are the main similarities in the arguments against sociology in Items C and D? (4 marks)

d) Give an example from the sociology you have studied of what Baker calls 'excuses for the inexcusable'. Give reasons for your choice. (3 marks)

e) With reference to the data here and the 'value-freedom' debate in sociology, assess Marsland's view in Item C that sociology is biased and one-sided. (10 marks)

Question 10 **Sociology and Science**

ITEM A **IS SOCIOLOGY A SCIENCE?**

When we ask, 'Is Sociology a science?', we mean two things: 'Can the discipline be closely modelled on the procedures of natural science?' and 'Can Sociology hope to achieve the same kind of precise, well-founded knowledge that natural scientists have developed in respect of the physical world?' These issues have always been to some degree controversial, but for a long period most sociologists answered them in the affirmative. They held that sociology can, and should, resemble science both in its procedures and the character of its findings.

(Anthony Giddens, *Sociology*, Polity Press, Oxford, 1989)

ITEM B **IN THE SHADOW OF SCIENCE**

...unlike the rocks, plants, and animals of the natural sciences, the subject matter of the social sciences – human beings – think. This awareness, or consciousness, about what is happening to them makes the subject matter of the sociologist extremely difficult to control. Sociologists cannot, for moral or practical reasons, carry out laboratory experiments very easily. Nor, given that sociologists... are also human, can they divorce themselves from the people or from the issues they are studying. It is not easy to be detached from the family when you have been brought up in one or are living in one on an everyday basis.

(Tony Lawson, 'In the shadow of science' *Social Studies Review*, vol. 2, no. 2, November 1986)

ITEM C WHO CONTROLS THE SCIENTIST?

('Science on our side', *British Society for Social Responsibility and Science*, 1983)

ITEM D HOW SCIENTIFIC IS SCIENCE?

Feyerabend not only admits nonrational elements into the scientific process but sees them as dominant. Science, he says, is an ideology, completely shaped at any moment in time by its historical and cultural context...There is no one scientific method, good for all times and places; in fact, there is no such thing as scientific method. Despite scientists' claims, the rule in science is that 'anything goes'.

(W. Broad and N. Wade, *Betrayers of Truth*, Simon and Schuster, London, 1982)

a) Is the author of Item A describing a positivist or phenomenological approach to sociology? Explain your answer. (4 marks)

b) Give three examples of the 'moral or practical reasons', referred to in Item B, why sociologists cannot carry out laboratory experiments very easily. (3 marks)

c) How have sociologists responded to criticisms of the use of the 'scientific method' such as those in Item B? (7 marks)

d) How does the cartoonist responsible for Item C attack the idea that natural science is objective and neutral? Give two examples to support his view.

(4 marks)

e) Using material from here and elsewhere, explain and discuss the statement in Item D that 'there is no one scientific method, good for all times and places...' (7 marks)

2 Education

Question 1 The Role of Education

ITEM A VOCATIONAL AND SPECIALIST EDUCATION

In any society there must be some adequate provision for instruction and training in all the tasks and skills of the social order, and in the various qualities (of mind, character, physical cababilities, etc.) required for their satisfactory performance. There must be an effective handing on of skills and related qualities if new generations are going to maintain and enjoy the previous achievements of their society, and if they are to have the opportunity of improving upon them. There must, in short, always be a practical, utilitarian (useful), technical and specialist kind of education in society.

(R. Fletcher, *Education in Society: The Promethean Fire*, Penguin, Harmondsworth, 1984)

ITEM B GOVERNMENT POLICY AND EDUCATION

The Conservative Government which came to power under Margaret Thatcher in 1979 sought to establish a more direct relationship between education and industrial and economic needs. The emphasis was now on reduced costs, and on value for money. If British industry was not adequately competitive, if the British economy was in difficulties, if British technology was out of date, then the answer was being sought in the schools and in further and higher education. Throughout higher education, government sought to divert students from the humanities and social sciences to the natural sciences and technology.

(Judith Ryder and Harold Silver, *Modern English Society*, 3rd edition, Methuen, London, 1985)

ITEM C WHY A NATIONAL CURRICULUM?

The government aims to introduce a National Curriculum which will ensure that all pupils get a broad, balanced curriculum which is relevant to their needs and set in a clear moral framework. This will prepare them better for the responsibilities required in adulthood. It is being introduced in an attempt to overcome the disappointingly low standards found in many of Britain's schools by setting clear targets and monitoring progress. Despite some good performance many children perform less well than their counterparts in other leading European countries. Teachers expectations are too low and the curriculum can often be narrow and unbalanced.

(Adapted from information leaflet, DES, London, 1988)

ITEM D AN IDEOLOGICAL APPARATUS

Althusser argues that the state 'is a machine of repression, which enables the ruling classes . . . to ensure their domination over the working class'. He asserts that this process operates both through the state's 'repressive apparatus' such as the police and the armed forces, and its 'ideological apparatus' such as education, the family and the mass media.

Althusser sees the school taking 'children from every social class at infant school age, and then for years ... it drums into them a certain amount of 'know-how' wrapped in the ideas of the ruling class'.

Schools exert a crushing blow to individuality and indoctrinate pupils into accepting class inequalities.

(Adapted from Philip Robinson, *Perspectives on the Sociology of Education*, Routledge and Kegan Paul, London, 1981)

---

a) What sociological perspectives are used in Items A and D? Briefly explain the reasons for your answer. (4 marks)

b) To what extent do the views of the Conservative Government in Item B reflect the view of the role of education as described in Item A? (3 marks)

c) Why do you think the Conservative Government attempted to 'divert students from the ... social sciences'? (3 marks)

d) Referring to Item C and data from elsewhwere, explain what factors influence the shaping of the curriculum. (7 marks)

e) Assess the basic ideas of the National Curriculum as outlined in Item C using any one sociological perspective. (8 marks)

Question 2 **The New Vocationalism**

ITEM A **VOCATIONAL TRAINING**

NOW that Royal Assent has been given to the Employment Bill, the MSC has become the Training Commission. Its objective is clear and vital – to ensure that Britain has a highly trained, highly motivated workforce.

The Training Commission will be an expanded body, to accommodate additional employer representatives, reflecting the growing demand from employers for skilled labour, which will need to be met through training.

The Commission expects to approach its task in such a way that training will become a way of life. The ability to learn will be as important as what is learned.

'Employment Training' is aimed at providing 600,000 adults per year with the chance of custom-designed training, to get those who have been unemployed for more than six months back to work.

To give all young people a positive introduction to the world of work, the TVEI (Technical and Vocational Education Initiative), helps 14-18 year olds apply their skills and qualifications to real life problems, as well as emphasising the value of enterprise, motivation and initiative.

(*Towards Employment Training*, Issue 1, Training Commission, Sheffield, June 1988)

ITEM B **TRANSFERABLE SKILLS**

In a good , or rather bad, proportion of the schemes I visited in South London, the trainees seemed to spend a lot of their time sweeping floors, cleaning up, running errands, etc. Clearly they were being taught how to lend a hand, make themselves useful and look sharp

– part of the traditional discipline of apprenticeship. Yet I was told that these trainees were actually mastering 'transferable skills' that would enable them to find work in a variety of occupations.

(Philip Cohen, 'Against the new vocationalism', in I. Bates et al., *Schooling for the Dole 1984*)

ITEM C TRAINING FOR ROUTINE JOBS

Although there has been vigorous debate about YTS, there is some underlying agreement about how it functions in relation to the economy. The Marxist, Paul Thompson, has argued that the main purpose of YTS is to produce a pool of workers who will be employed in low-paid routine jobs, largely in the service sector of the economy. Because of the sharp decline in better paid jobs in manufacturing industry, these jobs are the best that the great majority of YTS trainees can hope for. An MSC report on the first three years of YTS gives figures for the main areas of YTS training which seem to support Thompson. The four leading areas were:

Administrative, clerical and office...18%
Personal service and sales 17%
Manufacture and assembly 14%
Installation, maintenance and repairs..13%

(Mike O'Donnell, 'Education and Work', *New Society*, 11 March 1988)

ITEM D EDUCATION AND LABOUR MARKET STATUS OF 16-YEAR OLDS

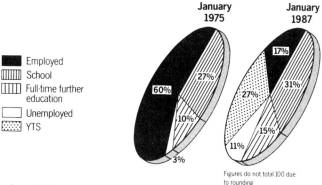

(*Employment Gazette*, September 1987)

a) What in Item A does the Training Commission (now known as the Training Agency) think **should** be the role of education? (4 marks)

b) Using evidence from Items B and C, and elsewhere if you wish, criticise the view in Item A that the objective of 'employment training' is 'to ensure that Britain has a highly trained, highly motivated work force.' (10 marks)

c) What are the main trends in the employment and education of 16 year olds shown in Item D and why do you think these have occurred? (6 marks)

d) What else in society apart from education might be affected by the changes shown in Item D? Give **one** example only and offer reasons for your answer. (5 marks)

Question 3 **The Hidden Curriculum**

ITEM A SOCIALISATION AT SCHOOL

When a child goes to school he or she is not only confronted with the traditional school subjects, but also with codes and pratices governing behaviour. The pupil has to learn not only history and geography, but also how to relate to teachers and fellow students: for example, when it is acceptable to claim the attention of the teacher and to ask questions, or when conversation with friends is allowed. He or she also has to learn which strategies are acceptable in which classroom, since teachers' demands will vary. Research seems to indicate that pupils are evaluated on their mastery of this 'hidden curriculum' just as they are evaluated on their mastery of the formal syllabus.

(Tony Bilton et al., *Introductory Sociology*, 2nd Edition Macmillan, Basingstoke, 1987)

ITEM B A COLLEGE PROSPECTUS

The distinct emphasis that we, as a Sixth Form College, would place is on helping students achieve **independence** . They are encouraged in all they do here to motivate themselves, to organise themselves, to develop their own values and beliefs and to lean on the support of others less markedly than was appropriate in the earlier secondary years . . .

Listed below are the skills, the concerns and the various kinds of awareness that we wish each of our students to acquire in the maximum:
1. Respect for the worth and dignity of all men and women, whatever their race, language nationality and creed.
4. The skills, personal and social, that are likely to lead to self-discipline and successful relationships with others . . .
9. An understanding of those communities, at home, at work, or in leisure in which our students are likely to find themselves, with a readiness to work constructively for the good of those communities.
10. A regard for healthy recreational activities and a willingness to participate in and promote these in the interest of human well being, co-operation and higher endeavour.

(Extract from a *Sixth Form College prospectus*, 1987)

ITEM C GENDER SOCIALISATION IN A PLAYGROUP

After our observations . . . it became clear that there was a relatively low probability that anybody would react when a girl hit. Seventy-five per cent of the time that boys struck someone else, or even moved their hand in that direction, teachers would intervene, most of the time with a 'loud' reprimand that everyone in the room could hear. Only twenty-five per cent of the time that girls were aggressive did teachers say anything and most often gave a 'soft' reprimand, audible only to the girl herself, when they responded at all.

. . . John learned that he can (1) get a tremendous amount of attention and (2) eventually get to share that tinker toy by hitting another child . . . For girls, there's no response. It just doesn't work very often. Teachers quite inadvertently seem to be strengthening the pattern they're trying to discourage in boys, while teaching girls that physical aggression is not effective.

(Lisa A. Serbin 'Teachers, peers and play preferences', in Sara Delamont (ed.) *Readings on Interaction in the Classroom*, 1984 Methuen, London)

Far too many of the children of the 'permissive generation' are disruptive, lawless and even amoral. A third of crimes are now commited by those under 17 . . .

   Of course it would be wrong to assume that such amorality is common to all British school children, or even that schools are primarily responsible. Nevertheless, schools must accept a share of the responsibility. First, because an overly child-centred approach has abandoned too many children to a fate without rules . . .

   . . . religious education needs to form part of the core curriculum and should lay down unambiguous standards of behaviour and good practice, discipline and pupil responsibility. What those moral guidelines should be will become the source of argument and even controversy. School uniform, a disciplinary code and prefectorial system, a school pioneer corps, its links with local charities and parents' groups, truancy, and even standards of hygiene should be set down.

(Anthony Coombs MP, *Times Educational Supplement*, 27 November 1987)

---

a) According to the author of Item A what else has a pupil to learn at school apart from the formal curriculum? (2 marks)

b) With reference to Item B explain how and why the hidden curriculum is likely to change between a school and a sixth form college. (5 marks)

c) How can research such as Lisa Serbin's be used to explain gender differences in educational achievement? (5 marks)

d) What does Anthony Coombs think should be the content and role of the hidden curriculum? (5 marks)

(e) Critically assess Anthony Coombs' view with reference to different views of the role of education in society. (8 marks)

Question 4 **Social Reproduction**

ITEM A **THE CORRESPONDENCE PRINCIPLE**

The educational system helps integrate youth into the economic system, we believe, through a structural correspondence between its social relations and those of production. The structure of social relations in education not only inures (accustoms) the student to the discipline of the workplace, but develops the types of personal demeanour, modes of self-presentation, self-image, and social-class identifications which are crucial ingredients of job adequacy. Specifically, the social relationships of education – the relationships between administrators and teachers, teachers and students, students and students, and students and their work – replicate the hierarchical division of labour . . . Alienated labour is reflected in the student's lack of control over his or her education, the alienation of the student from the curriculum content, and the motivation of school work through a system of grades and other external rewards . . . Fragmentation in work is reflected in the institutionalised and often destructive competition among students through continual and ostensibly meritocratic ranking and evaluation. By attuning young people to a set of social relationships similar to those of the workplace, schooling attempts to gear the development of personal needs to its requirements.

(S. Bowles and H. Gintis, *Schooling in Capitalist America*, Routledge & Kegan Paul, London, 1976)

ITEM B SCHOOL RULES AND ORGANISATION

IN a simple physical sense school students . . . are subordinated by the constricted and inferior space they occupy. Sitting in tight ranked desks in front of the larger teacher's desk; deprived of private space themselves but outside nervously knocking the forbidden staffroom door . . . surrounded by locked up or out of bounds rooms, gyms and equipment cupboards; cleared out of school at break with no quarter given even in the unprivate toilets . . .

The social organisation of the school reinforces this (teacher-pupil) relationship. The careful bell-rung timetable; the elaborate rituals of patience and respect outside the staffroom door where even cheeky comments are prefaced with 'sir'; compulsory attendance and visible staff hierarchies – all these things assert the superiority of staff and their world.

(Paul Willis, *Learning to Labour*, Saxon House, Aldershot, 1977)

ITEM C COUNTER-SCHOOL CULTURE AND SHOPFLOOR CULTURE

Counter-school culture has many profound similarities with the culture its members are mostly designed for – shopfloor culture . . . the central thing about the working class culture of the shopfloor is that, despite harsh conditions and external direction people do look for meaning and impose frameworks . . . This is the same fundamental taking hold of an alientation that one finds in counter-school culture . . . The masculinity and toughness of counter-school culture reflects one of the central locating themes of shopfloor culture – a form of masculine chauvinism. The pin-ups with their enormous soft breats plastered over hard, oily machinery are examples of a direct sexism . . .

Another main theme of shopfloor culture is the massive attempt to gain informal control of the work process . . . the men to all intents and purposes actually control at least manning and the speed of production. Again this is effectively mirrored for us by working class kids' attempts, with the aid of the resources of their culture, to take control of classes . . .

(Paul Willis, *Learning to Labour*, Saxon House, Aldershot, 1977)

ITEM D 'SKYVERS'

Teacher:	Doesn't anybody want to stay for their exams?
Cragge:	'Ands up all who wants to stay? (Everybody groans. No hands go up).
Colman:	No point in my stayin'.
Jordan:	'E's got an apprenticeship.
Colman:	My dad's in the print and 'e's gettin' me in.
Teacher:	But you could stay on at school and learn. You don't have to be content with a trade.

Jordan:	I'm going into the docks, it's a skill and a privilege.
Teacher:	Privilege?
Jordan:	I got two uncles in. You got to 'ave your family in the docks to get in.
Teacher:	Don't any of you want to be educated?
Cragge:	Look at you – you're educated and where did it get you – teaching!

(Barry Reckord, 'Skyvers' in Graham Stoate (ed.), *Themes from Life: A sampler of contempary drama*, Harrap, London, 1983)

a) In your own words and with reference to Item A, explain what is meant by the 'correspondence principle'. (5 marks)

b) How are the working class pupils in Item B prepared for their adult role as industrial workers? (5 marks)

c) What is meant by the statement 'working class kids attempt to take control . . . of classes'? How does this challenge the correspondence principle? (6 marks)

d) Using the evidence here and from elsewhere, explain the 'skyvers', (Item D) dislike of the education system. (9 marks)

Question 5 **Cultural Capital and Language**

ITEM A **LINGUISTIC CODES**

We can distinguish between uses of language which can be called 'context-bound' and uses of language which are less context-bound. Consider, for example, the two following stories which the linguist Peter Hawkins constructed as a result of his analysis of the speech of middle-class and working-class five-year-old children. The children were given a series of four pictures which told a story and they were invited to tell the story. The first picture shows some boys playing football; in the second the ball goes through the window of a house; the third shows a man making a threatening gesture; and in the fourth a woman looks out of a window and the children are moving away. Here are the two stories:

(1) Three boys are playing football and one boy kicks the ball and it goes through the window the ball breaks the window and the boys are looking at it and a man comes out and shouts at them because they've broken the window so they run away and then the lady looks out of her window and she tells the boys off. (Number of nouns: 13. Number of pronouns: 6.)

(2) They're playing football and he kicks it and it goes through there it breaks the window and they're looking at it and he comes out and shouts at them because they've broken it so they run away and then she looks out and she tells them off. (Number of nouns: 2. Number of prounouns: 14.)

With the first story, the reader does not have to have the four pictures which were used as the basis for the story, whereas in the case of the second story the reader would require the initial pictures in order to make sense of the story. The first story is free of the context which generated it, whereas the second story is much more closely tied to its context. As a result, the meanings of the second story are implicit, whereas the meanings of the first story are explicit.

It is not that the working-class children do not have, in their passive vocabulary, the vocabulary used by the middle-class children. Nor is it the case that the children differ in their tacit understanding of the linguistic rule system. Rather, what we have here are differences in the use of language arising out of a specific context. One child makes explicit the meanings which he is realizing through language for the person he is telling the story to, whereas the second child does not to the same extent.

(Basil Bernstein, 'Education cannot compensate for society', in E. Butterworth and D. Weir (eds) *The New Sociology of Modern Britain*, Fontana, London, 1984)

ITEM B MY LIFE IN TEN YEARS' TIME

Middle-class 15-year old boy's essay:

As I look around me and see the wonders of modern science and all the fantastic new developments I feel a slight feeling of despondency. This is because I am beginning to wonder who will be in control of the world in ten years time, the machine or man. Already men are being shot round earth in rockets and already machines are being built that will travel faster and faster than the one before. I wonder if the world will be a gigantic nut-house by the time I'm ten years older. We are told we will be driving supersonic cars at fantastic speeds, with televisions, beds, and even automatic driving controls. Do we want this, do we want to be ruled by machinery. Gone will be the time when the family go out for a picnic on a Sunday Afternoon, we will be whisked along wide flat autoroads, we will press a button in a wall and out will come a plate of sandwiches ready prepared.

(continues for another 120 words).

Working-class 15-year old boy's essay:

I hope to be a carpenter just about married and like to live in a modern house and do a ton of the Sidcup by-pass with a motorbike and also drinking in the Local pub.

My hobby will be breeding dogs and spare time running a pet shop. And I will be wearing the latest styles of clothes.

I hope my in ten years time will be a happy life without a worry and I have a good blance behide me. I am going to have a gay and happy life. I am going to work hard to get somewhere in the world.

One thing I will not do in my life is to bring disgrace and unhappiness to my family.

(Dennis Lawton, *Social Class, Language and Education*, RKP, London, 1968)

ITEM C CULTURAL CAPITAL

Bourdieu is one of the few Marxist sociologists of education to take seriously the relationship between home and school He is interested in the role of schools in transferring social and cultural inequalities from one generation to the next. And he employs two crucial concepts in his account of this process of reproduction: 'habitus' and 'cultural capital'.

There is an intended parallel between the idea of cultural capital and that of economic capital. The latter provides financial advantage when invested wisely, the former can provide educational advantage, and thus also, eventually, financial advantage, when invested in schooling. Bourdieu has identified the strategic use of education, as an alternative to financial investment, as a means used by certain social groups to ensure the maintenance of family status and economic position from generation to generation. The school accepts and takes for granted the cultural capital of the dominant social groups within society and proceeds as though it were equally distributed among all students. The subordinate groups, the working class, do not have cultural capital. They fail at school and thus the social hierarchies within society are perpetuated and reproduced.

(Stephen Ball, *Education*, Longman, Harlow, 1986)

---

a) What does Bernstein mean in Item A by 'context-bound' and 'less context-bound' language? (4 marks)

b) What further information would we need about Hawkins' research in Item A to be able to judge its reliability and to assess how representative it is? (5 marks)

c) Why might the middle class boy in Item B do better at school than the working class boy? (7 marks)

d) What does Bourdieu mean by 'cultural capital'? Give some example of 'cultural capital' and explain why it helps those who have it to do well at school. (9 marks)

Question 6 **Teachers and Pupils**

ITEM A **STEREOTYPING IN SCHOOLS**

Stereotypes are one form of categorisation and generalisation among humans. Like any form of categorisation they may serve an important and useful function in that they reduce the need for learning and help a person to anticipate how he might react to a member of that category. The stereotype goes beyond categorisation for it ascribes certain characteristics to members of the category . . .

(David Hargreaves, *Interpersonal Relations and Education*, Routledge and Kegan Paul, London 1975)

ITEM B **A SOCIOLOGICAL EXPERIMENT AT SCHOOL**

Rosenthal and Jacobson did their research in Oak School in San Francisco. All the children aged six to twelve, were given a test of intelligence; however, the teachers were told that the test would allow the researchers to predict those children who were likely to 'show an unusual forward spurt of academic progress' in the near future. At the beginning of the next school year the teachers were given the names of from one to nine children in their class who had attained high scores on the test; in fact the names had been selected at random.

All the children were re-tested up to two years after the original test. The results led Rosenthal and Jacobson to conclude that a favourable teacher expectation towards a child seemed to have a positive influence on their attainment. In the first grade of Oak School the 'experimental' children gained on average fifteen points over the scores of the 'control' children, and in the second grade a gain of nine points.

(Philip Robinson, *Perspectives on the Sociology of Education*, Routledge and Kegan Paul, London, 1981)

. . . teachers' judgements are not based simply on past achievement. I asked the teacher of one 'popular' subject what were her principles of exclusion. In making up the right number she employed three:

1. the 'best ones';
2. those who seemed to have the 'right' attitude;

and

3. from 3c, the three who seemed a 'cut above the rest';

It was no good having problem people like John Church.

'He's too lazy, he lays around, and if he gets his pen out, he lolls around saying 'Oh Miss!' I can't take the risk, it spreads like cancer. who starts it initiates it, I don't know.

It's cruel I know, but what else can I do? I haven't time to motivate, inspire, correct for behaviour and so on, you must cut out all the miscreants and thickies. You just haven't got time. They do drag you down. Now Sharon Brown, nice girl, parents didn't want her in that form, I think once she gets out and in with this other (more able) lot they'll pull her and the other two from 3c up.

(P. Woods, 'The myth of subject choice' in M. Hammersley, and P. Woods (eds), *Life in School,* Open University Press, Milton Keynes, 1984)

a) Which social groups are likely to be disadvantaged in the education system because of the 'stereotyping' mentioned in Item A? Explain why. (6 marks)

b) What criticisms could be made of the experiments carried out by Rosenthal and Jacobson (Item B). (5 marks)

c) Explain now the attitudes and actions of the teacher in Item C help us to understand differences in educational achievement. (6 marks)

d) What are the advantages and disadvantages of class-room based research as an approach to studying the problem of educational underachievement? (8 marks)

Question 7 **School Subcultures**

ITEM A **THE SOCIAL STRUCTURE OF CLASS 2TA**

Group H (5 boys)	Father's Occupation	End-of-year exam position	Detentions received	Socio-economic group
Max	Motor mechanic	6	14	3M
Donald	Factory worker	26	5	4
Peter	Crane driver	28	6	3M
Sammy	Docker	18	0	4
Nigel	Carpenter	20	1	3M

These five boys formed a close-knit friendship group; they were together in lessons, around the school and out of school. They were all working class boys with, except for Sammy, little interest in schoolwork; they were often involved in trouble in lessons and

frequently received school detentions . . . Their recorded offences included:
- caught on the building site
- misconduct in class
- missing English department detention
- climbing out of windows
- disruptive behaviour in Biology lessons.

(Stephen Ball, *Beachside Comprehensive*, Cambridge University Press, Cambridge, 1981)

ITEM B **OPPOSITION TO AUTHORITY**

The most basic and obvious dimension of counter-school culture is entrenched opposition to 'authority'. This feeling is easily verbalised by 'the lads' (the self-elected title of those in the counter-school culture).

(In a group discussion on teachers)
'(. . .) they're able to punish us. They're bigger than us, they stand for a bigger establishment than we do, like, we're just little and they stand for bigger things, and you try to get your own back. It's, uh, resenting authority I suppose.'

This opposition involves an apparent inversion of the usual values held up by authority. Diligence, deference, respect – these become things which can be read in quite another way . . . opposition is expressed mainly as style. It is lived in countless small ways, instantly recognised by the teachers, and an almost ritualised part of the daily fabric of life for the kids.

It is essentially what appears to be their enthusiasm for immediate authority which makes the school conformists – or 'ear'oles' – the second great target for 'the lads'.

(Adapted from Paul Willis, *Learning to Labour*, Saxon House, Aldershot, 1977)

ITEM C **IT'S DIFFERENT FOR GIRLS**

Like Paul Willis, I was using ethnographic research methods, involving a series of informal, loosely-structured interviews and systematic observation. However, when I attempted to use the 'gang of lads' model to understand young women's experiences, and to identify female versions of the lads and the 'earoles', I came up against a number of apparently insurmountable problems. At the most basic level, there was no clear similarity between the social structures of female and male friendship groups.

. . . Most young men 'hung around' in those 'gangs of lads' which have provided the foundation for so many studies of youth cultures and subcultures. Young women either had one extremely close 'best' girlfriend, or spent their time with a small group of two, three or four female friends.

. . . 'Deviance' for young women is usually defined in relation to their sexuality, so that to be labelled as a 'troublemaker' can be associated with being too feminine and too (hetero) sexual – a slag.

(Christine Griffin, 'It's different for girls', *Social Studies Review*, Vol. 2, No. 2, November 1986)

a) Explain what is meant by a 'school subculture', illustrating your answer with data from Item A. (5 marks)

b) Using evidence from the data here explain how school subcultures can affect the achievement of their members. (3 marks)

c) What are the similarities between the group in Item A and 'the lads' in Item B? (4 marks)

d) Using ideas in Item C, explain why Christine Griffin did not find female counter-school subcultures. (5 marks)

e) Why did Willis and Griffin use 'ethnographic research methods' and what criticisms can be made of ethnographic research in the study of education? (8 marks)

Question 8 **Education and Gender**

ITEM A **EXAMINATION RESULTS BY GENDER**

School leavers with higher grade results at 'O' level or CSE[1] in selected subjects: by sex, 1980/81 and 1986/87

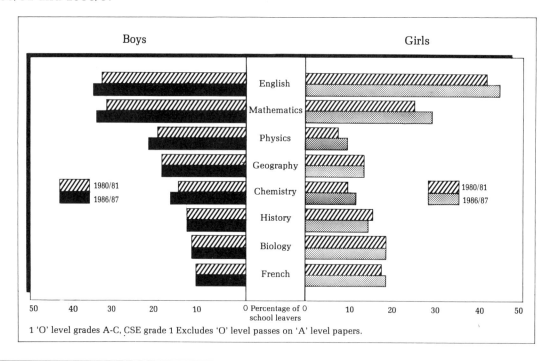

1 'O' level grades A-C, CSE grade 1 Excludes 'O' level passes on 'A' level papers.

ITEM B **EXPERIENCES OF CLASSROOM INTERACTION**

Female pupil: 'I think he thinks I'm pretty mediocre. **I** think I'm pretty mediocre. He never points me out of the group, or talks to me or looks at me in particular when he's talking about things. I'm just a sort of wallpaper person.'

Sections of the pupils' interviews were designed to elicit a picture of classroom life as seen through the eyes of the pupils. Each was asked a series of questions of the type: 'Which of these pupils does the teacher pay most attention to?' In pupils' experience, it is the boys who stand vividly in classroom interaction. Despite the fact that there are almost twice as many girls as boys in the seven classes, boys' names appeared nearly two and one-half times as often as girls.

Boys are, according to the pupils' reports, four times more likely than girls to join in discussion, or to offer comments in class. They are twice as likely to demand help or attention from the teacher, and twice as likely to be seen as 'model pupils'.

More importantly, it seems to pupils that boys receive the lion's share of teachers' attention and regard. Boys are, on pupils' accounts:
– Slightly more likely to be the pupils for whom teachers display most concern
– Twice as likely to be asked questions by teachers . . .
– Three times more likely to be praised by teachers (and slightly more likely to be criticised . . .)
– Three times more likely to be the pupils whom teachers appear to enjoy teaching.

(Michelle Stanworth, *Gender and Schooling*, Hutchinson, London, 1981)

ITEM C SINGLE-SEX SCHOOLS

Notre Dame High School is an all-girls Catholic comprehensive in Glasgow's West End. When I was there in the 1960s it was the Scottish equivalent of a convent grammar. In the early 1970s it turned comprehensive . . . Despite its success, Notre Dame, like a number of other schools in the region, is now ear-marked for closure. The local education authority wants to merge it with a local Catholic, mixed sex school . . . One Labour councillor has been heard to say that single-sex schools are 'an anachronism'. But research shows that girls benefit socially and academically from single-sex schooling.

. . . Is it not time that women and girls benefited from a little more upward mobility? Under the existing system only a tiny percentage of girls leave school with the kinds of qualification which will lead them into reasonably well-paid jobs. Instead, most girls have to look to a man to provide them with the basic requirements of life. It is for this reason that, following marital break-up, most women, irrespective of social class, slip into poverty. It is only with better qualifications that women can avoid the dependency trap.

(Angela McRobbie, 'Keep the girls from the boys', *New Statesman and Society*, 12 August 1988)

a) Describe the patterns of educational achievement as illustrated by the statistics represented in Item A. (3 marks)

b) Assess the strengths and weaknesses of Item B as an explanation of the educational underachievement of girls. (6 marks)

c) Briefly outline two sociological explanations of female educational under-achievement (other than that suggested in Item B). (7 marks)

d) Explain and assess Angela McRobbie's argument in Item C about the relationship between single-sex schooling and women's careers. (9 marks)

Question 9 Education and Ethnicity

ITEM A EDUCATIONAL QUALIFICATIONS

Percentages and thousands

Great Britain	Ethnic group					
	White	West Indian/ Guyanese	Indian	Pakistani/ Bangladeshi	Other[2]	All[3]
Highest qualification held (percentages)						
Males						
Higher	17		24	12	33	17
Other	47	36	34	21	37	46
None	36	58	42	67	30	37
Females						
Higher	14	16	15		23	14
Other	36	30	29	14	34	35
None	50	54	56	80	43	51
All						
Higher	15	12	20	9	28	15
Other	41	33	32	18	36	41
None	43	56	49	73	36	44
Sample size – (thousand) (= 100%)	22,559	229	352	194	283	23,881

1 Aged 25-59.
2 Includes African, Arab, Chinese, mixed and other non-white groups.
3 Includes those who did not state their ethnic groups.

(Social Trends 18, HMSO, London, 1988)

ITEM B THE CULTURE OF RESISTANCE: WEST INDIAN MALES

. . . the theme of reputation for masculinity provided the basis of their relationship with every aspect of school life.

A great many traditional activities were proscribed by the importance of being seen as hard and this often included playing sports for the school, even when the boys were good at it.

P: I used to do a lot (of sport) for the school, but I don't do it any more. I can't be bothered to do things after school, I'd rather go and watch and not take part.

This theme (of 'masculinity') was particularly influential in how they felt they should conduct themselves with teachers. Discipline was only acceptable to the boys if it did not compromise their sense of dignity.

Pursuing subcultural goals at school for these pupils was often a matter of appropriating private time . . . Of course, it was not possible to miss or turn up late for every lesson. These boys were acutely sensitive to those teachers with whom they could get away with it and those teachers they thought so little of that getting caught did not bother them. These boys seemed intent on exploiting every possible weakness in the school's armour to find time and space to celebrate their own cultural values.

Conflict was inherent in the very form of association the boys adopted. Establishing their public sense of identity as a group demanded that they be together and maintain an essentially school-based territory. They nearly always came to school, but in order to achieve identity they had to 'redefine' school time and space and this inevitably brought then into conflict with their teachers.

(John Furlong, 'Black resistance in the liberal comprehensive', in Sara Delamont, *Readings on Interaction in the Classroom*, Methuen, London, 1984)

ITEM C AFRO-CARIBBEAN GIRLS

Studies done in the 1960s found that girls of West Indian origin tended to perform better than boys in educational ability tests . . . A feminist interpretation was provided by Sue Sharpe in 1976. She studied a cross-section of 249 working class girls in the London Borough of Ealing, of whom 51 were of Afro-Caribbean parentage and 49 of Asian . . . unlike their white peers, they firmly believed that education and qualifications were important. She offered three explanations for this difference: parental support, positive attitudes to being female and an apprehension about leaving school.

For my own research, I interviewed ten black British girls, aged between 16 and 19, studying for A levels at two colleges of further education. Two of the fathers had white-collar jobs; two mothers were part time secretaries. The other eight mothers worked in low paid and insecure jobs and the fathers did skilled or unskilled manual work.

This was typical of the kind of comments made: 'My father wanted me to go for A levels. He says being black you won't get anything without education.' 'My father has always been very ambitious for us. He wants us to work hard at college so that we can get a good job'.

The young women I interviewed were all confident of their ability to achieve good results . . . All seemed to have good relationships with their college tutors and it was important to them to be viewed as good students. Education was a way of achieving independence, it was a commodity, which allowed them to enter relationships with men on equal terms.

(Ruth Chigwada, 'The education of the Afro-Caribbean girl', *New Society*, 4 March 1988)

ITEM D RACIAL STEREOTYPES

Even if they are not consciously, intentionally racist, teachers are not entirely free from prevailing racial stereotypes. These stock images include both Asian pupils ('they keep themselves to themselves') and West Indian pupils ('unruly and disruptive'). Clearly, if teachers are influenced by these stereotypes, and if they expect ethnic minority pupils to perform poorly, then this could have important consequences in such areas as streaming, examination entry, subject choice and careers advice. In a famous attack on teachers, one writer claimed that their belittling of black pupils damaged self-esteem: 'The black child's true identity is denied daily in the classroom. In so far as he is given an identity, it is a false one. He is made to feel inferior in every way. In addition to being told he is dirty and ugly and sexually unreliable, he is told by a variety of means that he is intellectually inferior. When he prepared to leave school, and even before he is made to realise that he and 'his kind' are only fit for manual, menial jobs'.

(B. Coard, 'What the British school system does to the black child', J. James & R. Jeffcoate, *The School in the Multicultural Society*, Harper & Row, London, 1981)

a) Identify the main patterns of educational achievement among ethnic minorities as shown in Item A. In your answer, refer to differences between males and females. (7 marks)

b) With reference to Items B and D, explain the relative failure of West Indian males in education. (8 marks)

c) How does Ruth Chigwada (Item C) explain the relative success of West Indian girls? (4 marks)

d) Evaluate Ruth Chigwada's research as described in Item C. (6 marks)

Question 10 **Public Schools**

ITEM A PUBLIC SCHOOLS AND THE ELITE

The army elite is dominated by those of public school education. In 1970, 86 per cent of officers of the rank of major-general or above had attended public school, a notably higher proportion than in 1939 (64 per cent). The most prestigious regiments remain extremely selective in terms of social class when recruiting new officers. Between 1976 and 1978, of 73 new officers entering the Guards or Royal Green Jackets 62 had attended a small group of high status public schools. Not one had attended a state school.

Assessed in terms of social origin and educational background, British judges are probably the most exclusive of all elite groups in Britain. Between 1960 and 1969 well over three-quarters of High Court judges received their education in Public Schools. Of the principal judges, 81 per cent received a public school education. A striking feature of the data is the number of the judiciary who were educated at one of a handful of major public schools.

(P. Abrams and R. Brown (eds), *UK Society*, Weidenfeld and Nicholson, London, 1984)

TOP SCHOOLS FOR TOP JOBS

	%
Conservative cabinet 1982	73
Conservative junior ministers 1982	88
Conservative MPs 1979	67
Labour cabinet 1979	21
Labour junior ministers 1979	21
Labour MPs 1979	8
senior civil servants 1970	62
Judges of the High Court and Court of Appeal 1971	80
Bishops of Church of England 1971	67
professors etc at Oxford and Cambridge 1967	49
professors etc at universities , England & Wales 1967	33
directors of 40 major industrial firms 1971	68
directors of major insurance companies 1971	83

In 1967, 2.6% of 14 year olds attended public schools.

NO CHANGE AT THE BANK

Directors of the Big Four banks educated at public school

	%	number
1927	76	62
1961	71	94(1)
1980	72	67(2)

(1) includes 38 to Eton (2) includes 25 to Eton.

(Stephen Fothergill and Jill Vincent *The State of the Nation,* Heinemann, London, 1985)

ITEM C **THE OLD SCHOOL TIE**

Dressed in long wigs, breeches and buckled patent shoes, Anthony Thornton and John Hand stood side by side in the Royal Gallery of the House of Lords last week.

They were to be sworn in as Queen's Counsels, a promotion likely to take them to the top of the barristers' earning leagues.

But their routes to the top and their social backgrounds are starkly different. Thornton is the son of an army officer and went to Eton and Oxford. Hand grew up in a terraced house in Huddersfield and went to a technical high school and Nottingham University; his father was a lorry driver.

Does this mean that the traditional elite profession of the bar is becoming more meritocratic? Last week the Sunday Times put it to the test by looking at the class background of the 57 new Q.Cs.

We found that Hand, with his working class background was very much in the minority and that QCs are still a non-meritocratic, self-perpetuating elite, drawing most of its members from public schools and Oxbridge.

Of the 54 new QCs we spoke to only 15 attended state schools, of those only four had been to comprehensives.

(Jon Craig, *The Sunday Times,* 17 April 1988)

'Advice to a younger brother', 14-year-old public school boy:

'Remember that the prefects do practically all the running of the house and their word is law'.

An elite of senior boys is an important agent of social control in the public boarding school. By formally awarding them privilege, the staff encourage them to identify with the perspective of the school and its official codes of conduct rather than the perspectives and codes of conduct of other boys.

The power of the prefects is predominantly based on the informal rewards and punishments which they are in a position to hand out and they act as both judge and jury.

There are in all public boarding schools, several levels of prefecture arranged in a hierarchy – the occupant of each office having authority over those 'below' him.

Sixth former, The Leys School:

'. . . a school prefect is a sound, reliable person who does his duty and can wear a school prefect's jacket, wear any tie he likes, use any umbrella and other meaningless status symbols . . . A House Prefect is someone like myself, who wasn't a reliable enough or good enough "chap" . . .'

(Adapted from John Wakeford, *The Cloistered Elite,* Macmillan, London, 1969)

---

a) Using Items A, B and C describe the relationship between the Elite (holders of top jobs) and the public schools. (6 marks)

b) What sociological explanations can you suggest for this relationship? Justify your answer. (7 marks)

c) Describe those parts of the Public School 'hidden curriculum' referred to in Item D. (3 marks)

d) How does the 'hidden curriculum' in Item D socialise public school pupils for their likely adult role? (4 marks)

e) What difficulties would there be in obtaining accurate data on public schools? (5 marks)

3 The Family

Question 1 **The Role of The Family**

ITEM A FUNCTIONS OF THE FAMILY

It seems possible to offer a summary statement of the more important functions of the family:

1. The family regulates sexual behaviour in relation to the satisfaction of both sexual needs and the achievement and maintenance of other desired qualities and relationships.

2. The family secures a legitimate and responsible basis for procreation and the rearing of children.

3. The family provides for the sustenance and care of its dependent members – whether children, aged, or those dependent for other reasons.

4. The family provides, in a continuing and detailed fashion, the earliest and most impressive education for the young. In so doing, it introduces the child to those values and modes of behaviour which are appropriate to all kinds of social activity both within and beyond the family. It accomplishes what is usually called the 'socialisation' of the child. Thus it serves as an important agency in the perpetuation of 'social traditions'.

5. Finally, since the 'titles' of the members of the family – 'husband', 'wife', 'eldest son' etc. – bear specific and different social connotations, the family can be said to invest its members with those rights, duties, customary and legal demands which are recognised and insisted upon in the community in which they live.

(Ronald Fletcher, *The Family and Marriage in Britain*, Penguin, Harmondsworth, 1962)

ITEM B EMERGENCE OF THE MODERN FAMILY TYPE

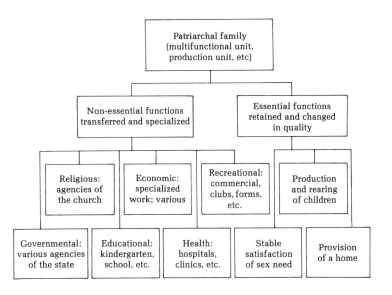

(Ronald Fletcher, *op. Cit.*)

Most Marxist analyses draw attention to the ways in which families tend to encourage and reproduce hierarchical inegalitarian relationships, and to act as a safety valve, dampening down discontent so that it is robbed of revolutionary content. In providing a place where children can be conceived, borne and reared in relative safety, the family is providing tomorrow's labour force. At the same time, by offering a centre for relaxation, recreation, refreshment and rest, the family helps to ensure that members of today's labour force are returned to work each day with their capacity to work renewed and strengthened.

(Tony Bilton et al, *Introductory Sociology*, 2nd edition, Macmillan, Basingstoke, 1987)

ITEM D **THE POLITICS OF THE FAMILY**

It is rare these days for a major political conference or rally to pass without some, and often quite extended, reference to the family. Of course, the family has always been an important element in political and social thought. However, there are probably several aspects of our recent history which have contributed to this 'rediscovery' of the family on the part of political leaders. These would include concerns about levels of public expenditure and the extent of state provision and the desire in some quarters to reduce these; the growth in long-term unemployment and the subsequent assumed consequences for family relationships; rising divorce rates; growing concerns about law and order; and the development of the 'pro-family' lobby especially, but not exclusively, among the 'New Right'.

(David Morgan, 'Sociology, society and the family', *Social Studies Review*, Vol. 2, No. 5, May 1987)

a) What is meant in Item B by 'Essential' and 'Non-essential' functions? (4 marks)

b) Referring to Items A and C how would Marxists criticise the functionalist view of the family? (6 marks)

c) How could recent evidence of the increased diversity of the British family be used to criticise Ronald Fletcher's view of the family expressed in Item A? (7 marks)

d) Using the evidence here and other sociological arguments, assess the view that the family is still an important social institution. (8 marks)

Question 2 **Socialisation**

ITEM A **THE FAMILY AS A SOCIAL GROUP**

The family provides an 'introduction', as it were, to the wider structure of society – to the knowledge of the wider pattern of kinship; the various groups and characteristics of the neighbourhood; the more detailed economic, governmental, educational, and religious organisations in society. In sociological terms the family is that most important **'primary' group** of society which gradually introduces the child to the complicated **'secondary' groups** of society – that complicated fabric of social organisation with which it will have to come to terms and within which it will have to work out the course and pattern of its life. Through this introduction, the family provides the child with those values and modes of behaviour which are appropriate for life in the wider society . . . the family is – for the child – the first, and perhaps the most important, agency of education in society.

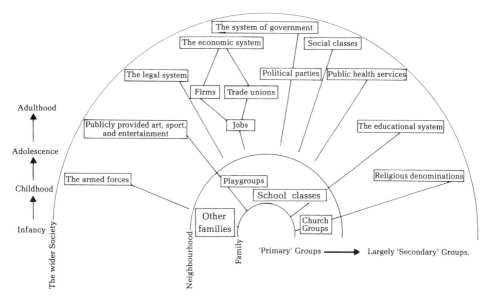

(Ronald Fletcher, *The Family and Marriage in Britain,* Penguin, Harmondsworth, 1962)

ITEM B **THE MOTHER AND CHILD CARE**

What is believed essential for mental health is that an infant and young child should experience a warm, intimate and continuous relationship with his mother in which both find satisfaction and enjoyment. It is this complex, rich, and rewarding relationship with the mother in early years, varied in countless ways by relations with the father and with the brothers and sisters, that child psychiatrists and many others now believe to underly the development of character and of mental health.

(John Bowlby, *Child Care and the Growth of Love,* Penguin, Harmondsworth, 1947)

ITEM C **GENDER AND SOCIALISATION**

Up to the age of about three both boys and girls identify with the mother. Then the little boy begins to develop an identity which is masculine. But because men are often not in the home at this time, the boy has to imagine a male role, this is usually done by rejecting anything which is 'feminine', including the mother. So little boys are often noisy and aggressive and see girls as inferior and 'cissy'. Training girls in the 'traditional' aspects of the female role is quite easy. They are drawn into helping their mothers, and practising this role is part of growing up.

A 14 year old girl talks about childhood socialisation:

'In most families the girl learns from a very young age that she must behave in a different manner from her brother, from the day she is given her first doll and is told she cannot go outside and play because it is raining and yet her brother can. Children learn how they are different from one another by the way the parents and their friends talk

41

about them. For example – "Oh what a sweet little girl you have and so pretty, does she help you around the house?" "What a rascal of a son you have, always getting into mischief."'

(Sue Sharpe, *Just Like a Girl*, Penguin, Harmondsworth, 1976)

a) Explain the terms 'primary group' and 'secondary group' used in Item A. (2 marks)

b) Why does Ronald Fletcher believe that the family is for children 'perhaps the most important agency of education in society'? (4 marks)

c) Suggest two implications for social policy of the view of the family expressed in Item B. (4 marks)

d) Using Item C and evidence from elsewhere explain how the family prepares boys and girls for adult roles. (6 marks)

e) Using evidence from here and elsewhere explain how sociologists have criticised the views about socialisation expressed in Items B and C. (9 marks)

Question 3 **Working Class Families**

ITEM A THE WIDER FAMILY

We were least prepared for what we found in the borough. The wider family of the past has, according to many sociologists, shrunk in modern times to a smaller body. The ancient family consisted not only of parents and their children but also of uncles and aunts, nephews and nieces, cousins and grandparents. Kindred were bound together throughout their lives in a comprehensive system of mutual rights and duties, which were almost as binding in the agricultural society of our own past as in some of the surviving primitive societies studied by anthropologists. But as a result of the social changes set in motion by the Industrial Revolution, relatives have, we are told, become separated from each other.

We were surprised to discover that the wider family, far from having disappeared, was still very much alive in the middle of London. We decided, although we hit on it more or less accidentally, to make our main subject the wider family.

(M. Young and P. Willmott, *Family and Kinship in East London*, Penguin, Harmondsworth, 1957)

ITEM B CONTACTS OF MARRIED MEN AND WOMEN WITH PARENTS

(*General sample – married people only*)

	Fathers		Mothers	
	Number with father alive	Percentage of those with father alive who saw him in previous twenty-four hours	Number with mother alive	Percentage of those with mother alive who saw her in previous twenty-four hours
Men	116	30%	163	31%
Women	100	48%	155	55%

(M. Young and P. Willmott, *Family and Kinship in East London*, Penguin, Harmondsworth, 1957)

ITEM C **FAMILY CONTACTS**

If one looks, in the 1980s, not at the **proximity** of relatives but at **contacts** between them, a different picture comes into focus. A number of recent surveys has shown that between about two-thirds and three-quarters of people – people of all ages, not just the elderly – see at least one relative at least once a week. I recently completed a study of married people with young children in a North London suburb, a district where as many as a third of the couples had moved in within the previous five years. There, the proportion seeing relatives at least weekly was precisely two-thirds. Of those with parents alive, one in ten saw their mother or father or both every day, and nearly two-thirds of living parents and parents-in-law were seen at least once a month.

(Peter Willmott, 'Urban kinship past and present', *Social Studies Review*, Vol. 4 No. 2, November 1988)

ITEM D **EASTENDERS**

(The BBC Soap) *Eastenders* is set in a largely working-class neighbourhood in the fictional borough of Walford in London's East End. It focuses on the relationships of a fairly enclosed community of characters. At the centre of the serial is a large extended family headed by the matriarchal figure of Lou Beale[1] . . .

Lou: I've been round this square longer than any of you. And in the old days, we used to be in and out of each other's houses and in and out of each other's business.

Ethel: That's right. You couldn't sneeze in the Square without everyone knowing about it.

Lou: But now all that's changed. You're supposed to keep yourself to yourself. That's progress, eh? It means that an old geezer like Reg Cox can lay dying in his flat and nobody notices.

   At the same time, *Eastenders* also refers to more modern notions of urban community, which emphasise social diversity, both in terms of class and ethnicity – in a sense, to the notion of the multicultural community . . . In several respects, the inner-city community of the mid-1980s may be seen as a site of considerable social tension – between the white working-class and the first- or second-generation immigrants who have increasingly been the victims of racist attacks; between the (rapidly declining) employed working-class and those who are unemployed, or operating in the so-called 'black economy'; and, most recently, between the indigenous community and the middle-class intruders who have sought to 'gentrify' their areas.

(1) Lou Beale has since been written out of the script.

(David Buckingham, *Public Secrets: Eastenders and its audience*, BFI, London, 1987)

a) What are the two types of family structure referred to in Item A?   (2 marks)

b) Describe the patterns of family contact shown in Item B.   (2 marks)

c) Using the evidence in Items A and B and from elsewhere assess the functionalist view that industrialisation leads to the creation of isolated nuclear families.   (8 marks)

d) How does the working-class family in the 1980s, depicted in *Eastenders*, differ from that described by Young and Willmott in the 1950s?   (5 marks)

e) What explanations are there for these differences? In your answer you should refer both to social changes and the sources of the data in A and D.   (8 marks)

Question 4 **The Diverse Family :1**

ITEM A PEOPLE IN HOUSEHOLDS BY TYPE OF HOUSEHOLD

Great Britain			Percentages	
	1961	1971	1981	1987
Type of household				
Living alone	3.9	6.3	8.0	9.9
Married couple, no children	17.8	19.3	19.5	21.5
Married couple with dependent children	52.2	51.7	47.4	44.1
Married couple with non-dependent children only	11.6	10.0	10.3	11.8
Lone parent with dependent children	2.5	3.5	5.8	4.7
Other households	12.0	9.2	9.0	8.0
All households	100	100	100	100

(*Social Trends 19*, HMSO, London, 1989)

ITEM B DIVORCE AND CHILDREN

That more couples are cohabiting, either as a preliminary or as an alternative to marriage, is one trend that has become firmly established since the seventies. Another has been the rising rate of second and third marriages. Higher divorce rates, on which the trend of course depends, were largely a function of new legislation, permitting divorce by consent and shorter waiting periods.

Divorce not only affects married couples and reflects their ideals about married life; it also affects others, especially children . . . The disturbing fact, from the children's point of view, is that in 1981 six out of every ten couples divorcing had children under sixteen, two-thirds of whom were under 11 and a quarter of whom were under 5 at the time of the divorce. Some of these children are likely to have been fairly quickly absorbed into 'reconstituted' families when their parents remarried. However, many more may have found themselves part of what officials have been pleased to call 'single-parent' families.

(Judith Ryder and Harold Silver, *Modern English Society*, 3rd edition, Methuen, London, 1985)

ITEM C THE ATTENUATED EXTENDED FAMILY

. . . this leaves under half the population for whom kinship is less important. Their type of arrangement might be called **the attenuated extended family.** The people concerned include students and other young people, both those who are single and young couples before they have any children of their own. They are at a stage when they are, as they need to be, breaking away from their family of origin – when kinship matters less, and their age peers more, than at any other phase in life.

   Most keep in touch with parents, adult children, brothers and sisters by letter or telephone; most do meet them, if only at Christmas, at rites of passage like marriages and funerals, and on one or two other occasions each year. For most, too, relatives provide mutual help, if not on a continuing basis, at least in times of need: parents lend their children money; children go to give help when a parent falls ill; parents, particularly mothers, travel to give their support in illness or at childbirth.

(Peter Willmott 'Urban kinship past and present', *Social Studies Review*, Vol. 4, No. 2, November, 1988)

ITEM D KINSHIP AND THE ECONOMY

The Ewing Family (from the American soap *Dallas*) is useful for reminding us of the continuing close relations between kinship patterns and the economy. Much sociological analysis, following Parsons, has tended to stress the separation between the kinship system and the industrial capitalist system. However, what this account frequently neglects, and what some soaps can properly remind us of, is the continuing influence of family and kinship in the new industrial capitalist societies.

   Just think for a moment of the famous family names of American capitalism – families which were and are dynasties: the Hunts, the Rothschilds, the Fords, the Carnegies, the Gettys.

(John Hood Williams, 'Dallas and the family', *Social Science Teacher*, Vol. 16, No. 3, 1987)

a) What are the main changes in family structure indicated by the data in Item A? (4 marks)

b) How would you explain the changes you described in answer to question (a)? (4 marks)

c) What family structures are described in Item B? (3 marks)

d) What is meant by 'close relations between kinship patterns and the economy' in Item D? (5 marks)

e) Using the evidence in Items C and D, and from elsewhere if you wish, assess the view that the extended family is no longer important in modern Britain. (9 marks)

Question 5 **The Diverse Family :2**

ITEM A HOUSEHOLDS WITH CHILDREN HEADED BY A LONE PARENT

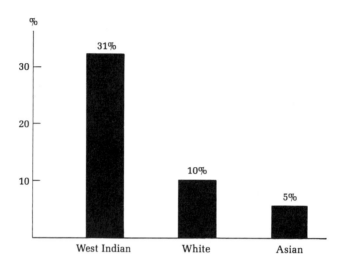

(Adapted from C. Brown, *Black and White Britain: the Third PSI Survey*, Heinemann, London, 1984)

ITEM B **MATRIARCHAL FAMILIES**

West Indian life is matriarchal or mother-centred and this is connected to slavery . . .
During slavery the nuclear family in particular was not encouraged by plantation owners –
this would have caused a solidarity which they did not want. And so family life for the
slaves was continually disrupted, the men were often forcibly taken away from their
families and it fell upon the women to maintain and control the family. So, if West Indian
life is . . . matriarchal it is slavery and tradition that has made it so.

(J. Breeze, 'A family of women', 1985, in Diana Leonard and John Hood-Williams, *Families*, Macmillan, Basingstoke, 1988)

ITEM C **IMAGES OF THE FAMILY**

The supermarket image of the British family beams from cornflake packets and the banks.
It is an image of a white middle class family, a wife and husband and two children, a boy
and a girl. This, it suggests, is a normal family and black families of Asian or Afro-
Caribbean descent, one-parent families or extended families are all abnormal.

Generally, Asian households (defined as those sharing food and shelter) are larger, with
4.6 members, than 'white' or 'West Indian' households with 2.3 and 3.4 members
respectively. Seventy three per cent of Asian households include children (the figure is 31
per cent for 'white' and 57 per cent for 'West Indians'). Among these, Muslim, Pakistani
and Bangladeshi households are likely to be larger, but they are not more likely to be
extended families. Households including more than one generation or where brothers and
their wives live together, which sometimes means that adjoining houses are knocked
together, are more common among Sikhs and East African Asians. Overall, however, the
proportion of extended families living together is 21 per cent – higher than among other
groups . . .

The trend, in fact, is towards nuclear families but this does not mean that the importance of extended family ties has diminished. On the contrary, economic and material assistance as well as emotional support are found in these enduring links. To say, as many Asian people do, 'We are family people' expresses a truth and a commitment to family life shown in the Sunday gatherings where food and news and the warmth and support of family members are shared across generations and households. People will travel miles to be together for family events, crammed into cars or into minibuses for the journey.

(Sallie Westwood and Parminder Bhachu, 'Images and realities', *New Society*, 6 May 1988)

a) How useful is the argument presented in Item B in explaining the statistics in Item A? What other explanations might be used? (8 marks)

b) According to Item C how is our image of the nuclear family as 'normal' reinforced? (3 marks)

c) Using evidence from Item C explain why the proportion of cohabiting extended families is higher in the Asian community than elsewhere. (7 marks)

d) What problems might a sociologist face attempting to research ethnic minority families? How might these problems be overcome? (7 marks)

Question 6 **The Family and Unemployment**

ITEM A CONJUGAL ROLES

When they were interviewed, six months after Phil had lost his job as a blacksmith in a dockyard, it seemed that they were in a state of crisis. Phil was depressed, bored and irritable.

While Wyn, his wife, was at work, Phil spent a large part of the day with his extended family. He described them as 'being company'. It appears that it was a secure place to be as his father and brother had had similar experiences and were out of work. This was no doubt the major source of support for Phil as he had contact with very few people outside his family at this time.

Once Phil returned to work, it seemed that conjugal roles would return to their original pattern – more segregated and unequal with Phil being the dominant partner. But as they had the experience of Wyn being the stronger and Phil being dependent on her, it would be inevitable that their relationship would be less polarized, that it would be more balanced, with a greater degree of flexibility in their roles of husband and wife.

(Leonard Fagin and Martin Little, *The Forsaken Families,* Penguin, Harmondsworth, 1984)

ITEM B ROLE BARGAINING

Goode applies the concept of **role bargaining** to his study of the family. This means that the individual attempts to obtain the best possible 'bargain' in his relationship with others. He will attempt to maximise his gains. In terms of family relationships, this means he will maintain relationships with kin and submit to their control if he feels he is getting a good return on his investment of time, energy and emotion.

(Michael Haralambos, *Sociology : Themes and Perspectives,* Unwin Hyman, Slough, 1980)

So, one of the first things you notice in Northern cities hit by unemployment is babies, lots of babies, with very young parents. Unemployed men in denims and trainers pushing buggies. The sight of teenage fathers is striking because it is in such stark contrast with the role of their own fathers, who weren't seen pushing prams when they were nineteen. You don't notice the young mothers so readily, because they're doing what they've always done. The real change is that many are doing it alone. Men come and go in their lives, but there is no necessary connection between motherhood and marriage. They are going it alone . . . because it is an alternative to aimless adolescence on the dole.

'Having a baby makes me feel a lot older and more mature. At first my mam and dad weren't pleased about me falling pregnant, and they used to go on about how I was going to manage. The bloke denied it was his, I felt awful though there's plenty have kids on their own round here.'

One of the women on this Sunderland estate told me they all recognise the drive:

'It's part of becoming a member of the community instead of just a reckless teenager. You don't need to get a job, when you're a mam. When you're a mam somebody **needs** you.'

(Beatrix Campbell, *Wigan Pier Revisited; Poverty and Politics in the 80s*, Virago, London, 1984)

> a) What effect did unemployment have on the conjugal roles of the family described in Item A? (3 marks)
>
> b) Using Goode's concept of 'role bargaining' explain how and why family structure is affected by unemployment. (8 marks)
>
> c) Explain why Beatrix Campbell in Item C thinks that unemployment might encourage young women to have babies. (4 marks)
>
> d) What sociological research methods have been used to collect the data in Items A and C and to what extent are these methods useful in making generalisations about the family? (10 marks)

Question 7 **The Woman's Role**

ITEM A **IMPACT OF INDUSTRIALISATION**

Industrialisation has had these lasting consequences: the separation of the man from the intimate daily routines of domestic life; the economic dependence of women and children on men; the isolation of housework and childcare from other work. Today's housewife can, and does, leave the four walls of home for factory, office, school, hospital or shop, but her world is **permanently divided from the world of men.**

While nine out of ten women (in a Britisih survey) who were not employed were housewives, so were seven out of ten of those with a job outside the home. Housework is clearly the major occupational role of women today. Employment does not itself alter the status (or reduce the work) of being a housewife.

Housewives in the urban British sample studied by the author in 1971 reported an average of 77 hours weekly housework. The amount of time housework takes shows no tendency to decrease with the increasing availability of domestic appliances, or with the expansion of women's opportunities outside the home.

(Ann Oakley, *Housewife*, Penguin, Harmondsworth, 1974)

ITEM B THE DIVISION OF LABOUR IN MARRIAGES

	Where both partners are doctors: proportion of doctors reporting that they undertook the task alone	
	Female doctors (%)	Male doctors (%)
Shopping	85	1
Arranging social activities	39	4
Household repairs	10	71
Cooking	81	1
Housecleaning	51	1
Looking after sick child	80	2

(M. Elston, 'Medicine: Half our Future Doctors?'; adapted from.
M. Webb, 'The Labour Market', in I. Reid and E. Wormald (eds),
Sex Differences in Britain, Grant McIntyre, London, 1982)

ITEM C WORKING ARRANGEMENTS

To find out our respondents' views, we asked them to use the following categories of possible working arrangements in families with children:

1 **Traditional –**   father working full-time and mother at home.
2 **Compromise –**   father working full-time and mother working part-time.
3 **Equality –**   both parents working full-time or both working part-time.

Respondents of different ages were asked which of the working arrangements they thought was best for a family with children under five and for a family with children in their early teens.

	Age			
	18-24	25-34	35-44	45+
	%	%	%	%
Preferred working arrangements for parents with children under 5 years old:				
'Traditional'	52	71	78	84
'Compromise'	36	19	12	13
'Equality'	10	7	3	1
For parents with children in their early teens:				
'Traditional'	8	11	12	28
'Compromise'	49	63	66	60
'Equality'	42	23	15	9

(Roger Jowell et al. *British Social Attitudes*, Gower, Aldershot, 1987)

> a) What does Ann Oakley mean in Item A when she says that the housewife's world 'is permanently divided from the world of men'? **(3 marks)**
>
> b) Why might the researchers in Item B have chosen male and female doctors to study the division of labour in marriages? **(4 marks)**
>
> c) What does the evidence in Item C tell us about attitudes towards the roles of men and women when their children are either under 5 or teenagers? **(8 marks)**
>
> d) Using the data here and from elsewhere assess the view that the roles of men and women in the family are becoming increasingly equal. **(10 marks)**

Question 8 **The New Man**

ITEM A **CHANGING ROLE OF MEN**

. . . seventy years ago, working men typically lived in local occupationally homogeneous communities, of which mining and dock work were the classic examples. Such communities evolved essentially male public organisations – the pub, the betting-shop, the football club: organisations which loosened marriage bonds and took resources away from women and children. But the newer patterns of inter-war industry around London and Birmingham, in the Home Counties and the Midlands, took their toll of the older male domination – reducing class solidarity perhaps and inviting more romantic love certainly. Particularly after the Second World War, hours of work were reduced, holidays lengthened, home ownership became more common, children were less ever-present, and men were drawn into a more intimate and longer spousehood than their predecessors had ever known. We have stated that privatization was a key description of the affluent worker in Luton by the 1960s. It involved a closer, more co-operative, domesticity for millions of men.

(A. H. Halsey, *Change in British Society,* 2nd edition, Oxford University Press, Oxford, 1981)

ITEM B **FAMILY LIFE IN EAST LONDON**

(An extract from a study which looked at the family in the London boroughs of Bethnal Green and Woodford, predominantly working class and middle class respectively, almost 25 years after Willmott and Young's classic study of family life).

One striking difference was how home-centred most Bethnal Green families had now become. In the 1950s, this had been a feature of the Woodford families. Mothers with a three month old child are, of course, likely to spend more time in the home than outside it. But it was noticeable how many husbands in Bethnal Green today were almost as much around, when they could be, as Woodford husbands. Do-it-yourself, even in rented property, and television – not to mention the baby – were clearly strong competitors of the pub and the football ground.

(Anthea Holme, 'Family and homes in East London', *New Society,* 12 July, 1985)

ITEM C **HUSBANDS HELP WITH HOUSEWORK AND CHILDCARE**

One of the first facts that emerged is that husbands (and wives) commonly make a distinction between housework and childcare: the degree of sharing in one area may be quite different from the degree of sharing in the other.

	No. of respondents	Housework			Childcare		
		High	Medium	Low	High	Medium	Low
working class	20	2	1	17	2	8	10
middle class	20	4	9	7	8	4	8

(Ann Oakley, 'Are husbands good housewives?' *New Society*, 17 Feb 1972)

ITEM D THE MASCULINE ROLE

A lot of research has concentrated on the experiences of girls growing up and the development of femininity, and has pointed to the need for changes in girls' upbringing, but boys' development is equally important if we are to succeed in changing both women's and men's roles. Throughout the course of growing boys learn and internalise a separate 'masculine' role and identity. Some of the mothers I talked to were aware of this and were trying to bring up their children, especially their sons, to take their share of household tasks:

'Sometimes I won't make the boys' beds and I feel rotten, and – oh well, I'll make it. Kevin turned round once and said, "It's a woman's job is that," and I said, "You pretend you're a woman then and go and do it." I said he's going to die of shock when he gets married because they're not like we were. We were brought up to do it, but these girls now aren't, so he's in for a nice shock.'

(Sue Sharpe, *Double Identity: The Lives of Working Mothers*, Penguin, Harmondsworth, 1984)

a) Referring to Item A, explain why in traditional working class communities men and women led separate lives. (3 marks)

b) What reasons does Halsey give (Item A) for men becoming increasingly home-centred? (3 marks)

c) Describe the relationship between class and husband's participation in house-work and childcare, indicated by Item C. Suggest one explanation for the differences between the behaviour of working class and middle class husbands (7 marks)

d) What methods could sociologists use researching the domestic role of men and what problems might they face? (7 marks)

e) Evaluate the sociological data contained in Item C. (5 marks)

Question 9 The Family: Childhood and Youth

ITEM A CHILDHOOD

The starting point of this article is the **social construction of childhood** itself: childhood – as so much recent sociological literature has made clear in the case of youth – differs greatly according to time and place and at some times, does not exist at all.

The writer most influential in charting the emergence of 'childhood' was the French demographic historian, Philippe Aries . . .

'In medieval society' wrote Aries, 'the idea of childhood did not exist . . . as soon as the child could live without the constant solicitude of his mother, his nanny or his cradle rocker he belonged to adult society.'

(Stephen Wagg, 'Perishing kids? The sociology of childhood', *Social Studies Review,* Vol. 3 No. 4, March 1988)

ITEM B YOUTH AND THE MEDIA

Newspaper articles were headed 'Facing the facts about youth', 'What's wrong with young people today' or (as in foreign papers) 'British youth in revolt'. Numerical estimates are difficult to make but somewhere near a half of the opinion statements expressed this theme. As usual, the popular press provided an archetypal statement:

'For years now we've been leaning over backwards to accommodate the teenagers. Accepting meekly on the radio and television that it is THEIR music which monopolises the air. That in our shops it is THEIR FADS which dictate our dress styles . . . we have watched them patiently through the wilder excesses of their ban the bomb marches. Smiled indulgently as they've wrecked our cinemas during their rock and roll films . . . But when they start dragging elderly women around the street . . .' (*Glasgow Sunday Mail,* 24 May 1964).

(Stanley Cohen, *Folk Devils and Moral Panics,* Granada, St. Albans 1972)

ITEM C TIME TO LEAVE HOME

Much low-cost public and private housing has been built with the 'typical' – now increasingly untypical – family in mind; a young couple and two small children. As a father of three unmarried children in their early twenties remarked: 'These houses weren't built for five adults.' And to marry and remain in the parental home is not considered satisfactory or appropriate by either party. Young people expect a home of their own, and many parents, even when space is ample, look forward to time on their own when their children are grown up and off their hands.

Contrary to popular belief, surveys show that most young people and their parents live amicably together. But tensions can arise from parents' sense of duty, obligation, concern and love. Thus in parents' attempts to encourage a persistent search for work, on which they know a 'proper' life rests, there are fine graduations between joking, nagging, criticism and condemnation.

(Patricia Allatt, 'Time to leave?', *New Society,* 1 April 1988)

ITEM D CHILDREN AND FAMILY DECISIONS BY SOCIAL CLASS

Suppose a big decision is being made in your household, what do you think should happen?
Parent(s) decide and tell the child(ren) afterwards
Parent(s) decide after discussing with the child(ren)
Everyone discusses it and the family decides together.

	Social Class			
	1/2	3NM	3M	4/5
	%	%	%	%
A (Parents decide)	24	22	29	26
B (Discussion then parents decide)	40	29	24	22
C (Joint decision)	31	45	44	50

(Roger Jowell et al, *British Social Attitudes,* Gower, Aldershot, 1987)

---

a) Briefly explain what is meant in Item A by the 'social construction of childhood'. (3 marks)

b) Why does the media often present a negative view of youth as in Item B? (4 marks)

c) What are the sources of conflict between the generations suggested in Item C? (3 marks)

d) Describe and explain the relationship between social class and the role of the child in Item D. (7 marks)

e) Using any of the evidence here or from elsewhere assess the view that the role and status of the child is socially determined and not simply the consequence of age. (8 marks)

Question 10 **Marital Breakdown**

ITEM A THE END OF MARRIAGE

In the 1970s the main debate over divorce statistics was between those who believed that they signalled the end of marriage and those who believed they marked an increasing demand for a higher standard of marital relationship, because they showed people's refusal to tolerate bad marriages. this debate is now largely over. It is now commonly recognised that **marriage as such is not about to end,** since divorce rates, though still high, are matched by high re-marriage rates.

(Diana Leonard and John Hood-Williams, *Families,* Macmillan, Basingstoke, 1988)

Period	First marriages		Remarriages		Divorces
	Number marrying per 1,000 single population aged 16 and over		Number remarrying per 1,000 widowed or divorced population		Persons divorcing per 1,000 married population
	Bachelors	Spinsters	Men	Women	
1906-10	58.0	55.8	39.4	13.0	0.1
1911-15	61.8	58.7	39.2	14.4	0.1
1916-20	64.7	57.4	49.6	22.6	0.2
1921-25	63.5	55.2	42.3	14.6	0.4
1926-30	61.1	54.8	38.3	11.0	0.4
1931-35	62.6	57.3	36.2	9.6	0.5
1936-40	78.7	73.3	38.3	10.3	0.6
1941-45	71.2	67.6	41.2	12.2	1.0
1946-50	75.6	75.7	63.2	20.6	3.7
1951-55	75.9	76.8	55.4	16.1	2.6
1956-60	78.7	82.6	48.6	13.2	2.1
1961-65	75.6	83.6	50.9	13.3	2.6
1966-70	81.2	94.2	60.6	15.5	3.9
1971	82.7	97.6	71.5	18.6	6.0
1972	82.8	98.9	93.0	24.9	9.5
1973	76.8	91.9	87.7	24.7	8.4
1974	72.2	87.1	84.9	24.5	9.0
1975	69.6	84.9	84.0	24.8	9.6
1976	61.1	78.0	80.1	a24.1	10.1
1977	60.6	75.4	81.9	24.7	10.4
1978	60.2	74.8	84.2	26.2	11.6
1979	58.6	73.5	81.5	25.7	11.2
1980	57.2	71.9	78.8	25.4	12.0

(Adapted from *Social Trends,* HMSO, London, 1980)

ITEM C **WIFE BEATING**

'Wife-beating' has long been a recognised aspect of marriage, and women are usually loathe to report it because they fear it will only get worse, or because they obscurely believe that they are to blame, and because 'ousiders' are very reluctant to believe them or to interfere in a private matter. Even so, assaults by men on their wives account for as much as a quarter of all reported crimes of violence (Dobash and Dobash, 1977-78). Much the same reluctance to report applies to domestic rapes, and yet rape crisis centres find that among women coming to them a very large proportion have been raped by men who know their victims well: husband, boyfriends, fathers and uncles. In British law, despite feminist protests, rape by a husband still does not count as the criminal offence of rape – which means effectively that it is tolerated by the state. What all of this suggests is that family life is often far from being a haven of peace.

(Peter Worsley, *The New Introducing Sociology,* Penguin, Harmondsworth, 1987)

a) Explain the opposing interpretations of high divorce statistics mentioned in Item A. (3 marks)

b) Using statistics from Item B assess the claim in Item A that 'marriage as such is not about to end'. (4 marks)

c) Why are domestic assaults likely to be under-reported? (4 marks)

d) Evaluate the methods used here to measure the success or failure of marriage. What other methods could be used? (7 marks)

e) How has the Feminist perspective contributed to our understanding of the relationship between men and women? (7 marks)

4 Stratification

Question 1 **The Distribution of Wealth**

ITEM A **DISTRIBUTION OF WEALTH**

United Kingdom	Percentages and £s billion			
	1971	1976	1981	1985
Marketable wealth				
Percentage of wealth owned by:				
Most wealthy 1%	31	24	21	20
Most wealthy 5%	52	45	40	40
Most wealthy 10%	65	60	54	54
Most wealthy 25%	86	84	77	76
Most wealthy 50%	97	95	94	93
Total marketable wealth (£s billion)	140	263	546	863

(*Social Trends 18*, HMSO, London, 1988)

ITEM B **DISTRIBUTION OF INCOME**

United Kingdom					Percentages	
	Quintile groups of households					
	Bottom fifth	Next fifth	Middle fifth	Next fifth	Top fifth	Total
1976	0.8	9.4	18.8	26.6	44.4	100.0
1981	0.6	8.1	18.0	26.9	46.4	100.0
1984	0.3	6.1	17.5	27.5	48.6	100.0
1985	0.3	6.0	17.2	27.3	49.2	100.0

(*Social Trends 18*, HMSO, London, 1988)

The official statistics show that, over the last decade, the trend has been towards greater income inequality. Between 1976 and 1984 the original or market income of the bottom fifth of UK households dropped as a share of all market income from 0.8 to 0.3 per cent while the top fifth moved up from 44.4 to 48.6 per cent.

(A.H. Halsey, 'Britain's class society', *The Guardian*, 1987)

ITEM C **MILLIONAIRES**

Professor Bill Rubinstein is a leading expert on the origins of the British rich. Although there is no definitive list of living millionaires, we do have details of the wealth left by those who die, and so Rubinstein based his work on all those who died in 1984 and 1985 leaving a million pounds or more. Rubinstein's research shows that those whose fathers were wealthy businessmen or landowners still make up 42 per cent of the ranks of the millionaires. 43 per cent of all millionaires were left over £100,000, and a further 32 per cent inherited between £10,000 and £100,000. Of course at the time of inheritance many years ago, these sums were worth far more than they are now.

('Fortune', *New Society* in conjunction with LWT, 22 August 1986)

ITEM D MIDDLE CLASS WEALTH

Britain's middle classes, so long demoralised and impoverished, are about to grow rich once more.

Calculations by a British merchant bank, Morgan Grenfell, suggest that about half the middle-aged households in the country will inherit property typically worth £35,000 – more than three times the annual disposable household income of £11,000 a year. As the proportion of elderly owner-occupiers rises, so will the proportion of middle-aged inheritors. By the end of the century, property worth £9 billion (in 1986 prices) will be handed on each year. In South-East England, Granny will often leave her children a house worth well over £100,000.

('Growing rich again', *The Economist*, April 9 1988)

a) Describe the changing pattern in the distribution of wealth as illustrated by Item A. (4 marks)

b) In what ways do the figures in Item A not give a true picture of the distribution of wealth? (3 marks)

c) Suggest reasons for the trend described in Item B. (4 marks)

d) If 'Britain's middle classes... grow rich once more', suggest how this might affect their life-chances and life-styles. (5 marks)

e) Describe two different sociological approaches to explaining the distribution of wealth and income. (9 marks)

Question 2 The Nature of Class

ITEM A MARX'S VIEW

For Marx, classes are an aspect of the relations of production. Classes are constituted by the relationship of groupings of individuals to the ownership of private property... This yields a model of class relations which is in two parts: all class societies are built around a primary line of division between two opposing classes, one dominant and the other subordinate.

(Adapted from Anthony Giddens, *Capitalism and Modern Social Theory*, Cambridge University Press, Cambridge, 1971)

ITEM B STATUS GROUPS

With some over-simplification, one might say that 'classes' are stratified according to their relations to the production and acquisition of goods; whereas 'status groups' are stratified according to the principles of their consumption of goods as represented by special 'styles of life'.

(Hans Gerth and C. Wright Mills, *From Max Weber*, Oxford University Press, 1946)

ITEM C GOLDTHORPE'S CLASSIFICATION

Class 1	Higher professional and administrative; large managers and proprietors.	Service Class
Class 2	Lower professional and administrative; managers in small businesses; higher technicians and supervisors.	
Class 3	Routine non-manual.	Intermediate Class
Class 4	Small business owners, farmers, self-employed.	
Class 5	Lower grade technicians and supervisors.	
Class 6	Skilled manual workers.	Working Class
Class 7	Semi skilled and unskilled manual workers.	

(John Scott, 'Women and class theory', *Social Studies Review*, Vol. 3 No. 2, November 1987)

ITEM D BASIS OF THE GOLDTHORPE CLASSIFICATION

Goldthorpe bases his class scheme on the market and work situations of particular occupations. Each of his 7 classes combines occupations which are typically comparable in terms of market and work situations... market situation is concerned with source and size of income, promotion prospects and so on.

(Adapted from David Rose and Gordon Marshall, 'Social stratification', in Michael Haralambos (ed.), *Developments in Sociology*, Vol. 4, Causeway Press, Ormskirk, 1988)

ITEM E A SUBJECTIVE VIEW OF CLASS

The ownership of the Aston Martin automatically placed the young man in a social class far above mine; but that ownership was simply a question of money. The girl, with her even suntan and her fair hair cut short in a style too simple to be anything else but expensive, was as far beyond my reach as the car.
...for a moment I hated him. I saw myself, compared with him, as the Town Hall clerk, the subordinate pen-pusher, half-way to being a zombie, and I tasted the sourness of envy. I wanted an Aston Martin, I wanted an expensive shirt, I wanted a girl with a Riviera suntan – these were my rights, I felt, a signed and sealed legacy.

(John Braine, *Room at the Top*, Penguin, Harmondsworth, 1959)

a) With reference to Items A, C and D explain what criticisms a Marxist would make of Goldthorpe's classification. (4 marks)

b) In what ways does Goldthorpe's classification (Item C and D) take into account the idea of 'status groups' as described in Item B? (4 marks)

c) Using Items A and B discuss which view of social class is being expressed by the writer of Item D. (3 marks)

d) With reference to any one area of sociological research, explain what problems a sociologist might have in using Goldthorpe's classification. (6 marks)

e) From the evidence here and elsewhere, assess the view that social class remains the most important form of social stratification. (8 marks)

Question 3 **Social Mobility**

ITEM A **THE OXFORD SOCIAL MOBILITY STUDY**

The most recent major study of social mobility in England and Wales was conducted in 1972. Kown as the Oxford Mobility Study, it was undertaken by a group of sociologists at Nuffield College, Oxford.

The table below shows the main findings. The percentages in the horizontal rows (in the right-hand corner of each cell) compare the social class of sons with that of their fathers. Thus, taking all the sons whose fathers were in social class 1, 45.7% of these sons are themselves in social class 1, 19.1% in social class 2 and so on through to social class 7 in which only 6.5% of sons born into social class 1 are located. The figures in bold print, going diagonally across the table, indicate the extent to which sons share the same social class as their fathers. For example, 32.2% of all sons whose fathers were in social class 7 are themselves in that same class in 1972.

The percentages in the vertical columns (in the bottom left-hand corner of each cell) refer to the parental social class of the men found in each class in 1972. For example, of all the men in social class 1 in 1972, 25.3% have fathers who were in that class, 13.1% have fathers who were in social class 2 and so on. The bold figures show the percentage of men in each category who have the same social class as their fathers. For example, 36.6% of all the men in social class 7 are the sons of fathers from that class.

		Sons' class in 1972							
		1	2	3	4	5	6	7	Total
Fathers' class	1	45.7 25.3	19.1 12.4	11.6 9.6	6.8 6.7	4.9 3.2	5.4 2.0	6.5 2.4	100.0 (680)
	2	29.4 13.1	23.3 12.2	12.1 8.0	6.0 4.8	9.7 5.2	10.8 3.1	8.6 2.5	100.0 (547)
	3	18.6 10.4	15.9 10.4	13.0 10.8	7.4 7.4	13.0 8.7	15.7 5.7	16.4 6.0	100.0 (687)
	4	14.0 10.1	14.4 12.2	9.1 9.8	21.1 27.2	9.9 8.6	15.1 7.1	16.3 7.7	100.0 (886)
	5	14.4 12.5	13.7 14.0	10.2 13.2	7.7 12.1	15.9 16.6	21.4 12.2	16.8 9.6	100.0 (1072)
	6	7.8 16.4	8.8 21.7	8.4 26.1	6.4 24.0	12.4 31.1	30.6 41.8	25.6 35.2	100.0 (2577)
	7	7.1 12.1	8.5 17.1	8.8 22.6	5.7 17.8	12.9 26.7	24.8 28.0	32.2 36.6	100.0 (2126)
	Total	100.0 (1230)	100.0 (1050)	100.0 (827)	100.0 (687)	100.0 (1026)	100.0 (1883)	100.0 (1872)	(8575)

Categories by Goldthorpe classification
Source: J. H. Goldthorpe, 1980

(Adapted from M. Haralambos, *Sociology*: Themes and Perspectives, 2nd edition, Unwin Hyman, London, 1985)

ITEM B MALE OCCUPATIONS, PERCENTAGES

Males	1911	1951	1971
Managerial and professional	6.9	12.6	21.5
Intermediate	11.9	13.3	14.5
Manual	73.6	68.4	58.8

(J.H. Goldthorpe, *Social Mobility and Class Structure in Modern Britain*, Clarendon Press, Oxford, 1980)

ITEM C CROSS-CLASS FAMILIES

At first sight the evidence appears to be against Goldthorpe (who excluded women from his sample). In our study for example, in half of the cases where both the husband and wife were in paid employment, they occupied different class positions. However, Goldthorpe has never denied that this situation is common, but he has observed that in such cases it is generally the man who has the higher class position and the greatest commitment to the labour market. Certainly our data confirm that in most 'cross-class families' men have a higher class position. But is it true that men also have a greater commitment to the labour market such that the class behaviour of their wives is more determined by their husband's class position than their own? There is evidence from our study that this might be the case. For example, it would appear that the voting intentions of wives in paid employment is better predicted from their **husband's** class position than from their own. But not all the evidence vindicates Goldthorpe's claims. Most notably it is not the case that the current class positions of married women are dependent on that of the male 'family head'. Women's class positions depend on their own individual attributes, and especially their credentials, and not on any characteristic of their spouse.

(David Rose and Gordon Marshall, 'Social stratification', in M. Haralambos (Ed.), *Developments in Sociology Vol. 4*, Causeway Press, Ormskirk, 1988)

---

a) In what ways does the table in Item A show social mobility in Britain?

(4 marks)

b) Why is it important for sociologists to take account of both the horizontal and vertical sets of figures in Item A when studying social mobility? (5 marks)

c) Use the data in Items A and B to assess the view that 'inequality of opportunity exists but that the way to the top is by no means closed'. (7 marks)

d) Using Item C and evidence from elsewhere, criticise the research of the Oxford Mobility Study. (9 marks)

Question 4 **The Upper Class**

ITEM A IMPORTANCE OF THE UPPER CLASS TO SOCIOLOGISTS

Over the past two decades, sociologists in this country have given a great deal of attention to studies of the manual working class, and to the 'new' middle class, but they have paid much less attention to the upper echelons (levels) of the class structure. The lack is a striking one because there are various reasons why the upper sectors of the British class structure – and the changes which may have occurred, and be occurring there – are of particular interest in sociology.

(Anthony Giddens, 'Elites in the British class structure', in Philip Stanworth and Anthony Giddens, *Elites and Power in British Society*, Cambridge University Press, Cambridge, 1974)

ITEM B SOCIAL ORIGINS OF COMPANY CHAIRMEN 1900-1972

	Working class (%)	Middle class (%)	Upper class (%)	Unknown (%)	Total nos. of individuals
Clearing banks	—	3	74	23	74
Merchant banks	—	—	89	11	38
Miscellaneous manufacture	1	13	59	27	161
Breweries	2	11	75	12	55
Iron and steel	2	11	55	32	41
Railways	—	11	86	3	37
Shipping	—	10	67	23	21
Oil	—	13	47	40	14
Retail	—	32	21	47	19
Mean	1	10	66	23	460

In this study we set out to describe the social background of chairmen (occupying 460 chairmanships) of large corporations and banks over a time period of some seventy years. A sample of firms was constructed initially by selecting the largest industrial companies, by asset size, at a number of different years – 1905, 1926, 1948, 1953, 1966 and 1971. Using the *Stock Exchange Yearbook* names of company chairmen were identified from the turn of the century up to the present time. A range of sources was then combed in order to gather as much biographical information upon these individuals as possible.

(Philip Stanworth and Anthony Giddens, 'An economic elite: a demographic profile of company chairmen', in Stanworth and Giddens, *op. cit.*)

ITEM C SOCIAL ORIGINS OF MILLIONAIRES

Born to succeed? – the status of the millionaires' parents

Wealthy businessmen — 29%
Landed aristocracy — 13%
Higher professionals — 12%
Farmers — 9%
Lower professionals, clerical and salesmen — 10%
Small businessmen — 17%
Working class — 10%

Nigel Paige

Source : birth certificates of millionaires who died in 1984 or 1985

(*New Society*, 22 August 1986)

ITEM D A WEALTHY LIFESTYLE

Colin Woodhead, public relations consultant, was suffused with a post-Budgetary glow on Wednesday morning, the day after the Chancellor, Nigel Lawson had made him £13,000 a year better off by cutting taxes on the rich.

The Woodheads leave their £350,000 six-bedroomed, three-bathroomed house in South London separately each morning, he in his Renault 25, she in Le Car, both run on the company.

The house is perhaps the greatest beneficiary of their high income: 'We buy decorative antiques', Linda says. 'Glass, pretty things. Recently Colin's started collecting Victorian watercolours. We have an agreement that we never commit a sum of money to something without discussing it. If I see something really pretty – a little table or something that's

£200 or £300, that's all right. But to go and buy an armoire which would cost £1,500, well, then I'd go and ask Colin'.

('Balancing a budget windfall')

---

a) Suggest two reasons why, as Giddens states in Item A, sociologists have given more attention to the study of the working class than the upper class.   (4 marks)

b) What conclusions can be drawn from the data in Items B and C about upward social mobility?   (6 marks)

c) In what ways might the research described in Item B be criticised?   (4 marks)

d) With reference to Item D suggest how the culture of the upper class is likely to differ from that of the middle class.   (4 marks)

e) How might sociologists explain the existence of an upper class in Britain?   (7 marks)

Question 5 **Gender and Ethnicity**

ITEM A OCCUPATIONAL CLASS BY SEX AND ETHNIC ORIGIN

1982 (%)	Men			Women		
	White	West Indian origin	Asian origin	White	West Indian origin	Asian origin
Professional employer, manager	19	5	13	7	1	6
Other non-manual	23	10	13	55	52	42
Skilled manual and 'foreman'	42	48	33	5	4	6
Semi skilled	13	26	34	21	36	44
Unskilled	3	9	6	11	7	2

(*Employment Gazette*, Vol. 92 No. 6, HMSO, London, 1982)

ITEM B **PART-TIME WORKING**

Part-time working provides employers with a flexible and cheap form of labour for which they do not have to pay the full costs of the generation of that labour power. Increasingly, the use of part-time workers enables vulnerable firms to survive at a time of economic recession. However, for part-time workers themselves this form of work may represent a pragmatic response for those who, because of domestic commitments, are neither able nor expected to work full-time.

Part-timers may be taken on to work extra shifts when production is high – for instance twilight or evening shifts are often used – and, although this forms an alternative to overtime working for the employer, part-time workers are paid standard rates of pay whereas full-timers would be paid overtime or at least rates for unsocial hours...

'... a flexible labour force becomes available which can be precisely moulded to meet operational requirements. The active use of part-time labour can lead to a higher level of efficient manpower utilisation than is often achieved by firms which rely solely on a full-time labour force.' (From an employer's journal)

(Angela Dale, 'Part-time working: pragmatism or patriarchy?, in *Social Studies Review*, Vol. 1 No. 2, November 1985)

ITEM C THE RULE OF THE GANGMASTER

In Lincolnshire, gangs of farm labourers, often women, work for as little as £50 a week, they are controlled by gangmasters. While they toil, their masters grow rich; a system that smacks of feudal serfdom.

Pat Forman, a fearless woman in her fifties who worked 16-hour days as a ganger for years is a vigorous campaigner against the rule of the gangmasters;

'I went on the gang in 1976, grading potatoes in Spalding. I had five kids and we were having a hard time and there wasn't any other work about; you had to take what you could get. The day I started work, the gangmaster asked me if I would like to do a bit of overtime and I said yes. I thought it was a chance to earn a bit extra. Then he asked me if I would drive the van and I said I would. Soon I was working from 7.30 in the morning to 10 at night. I didn't have any choice. You had to put in the hours, you couldn't say you wouldn't work or you'd be told to 'Eff off up the road.'

Then I joined a union and I got some other women to join but one Friday morning the gangmaster came in and told me he wanted to see me outside the van. I guessed what was coming. He said I was finished. I was sacked because I knew too much.'

(Russell Miller, 'Rich harvest for the gangmaster', *The Observer,* November 1988)

ITEM D THE 'DUAL' MARKET

'Were discrimination to stop overnight', says Colin Brown, author of the 1984 PSI Report on racial discrimination, 'there could still be a worsening in black people's position.' This is because blacks are concentrated in the sectors (like manufacturing) and the jobs (the worst) that have been hit hardest by the economic recession. In the Bradford wool textile industry, the share of Asians in the workforce peaked just as the recession began.

New job trends will work against black people. Research at Sussex University suggests that companies are moving to a 'dual market' jobs policy. They want an inner core of highly paid professionals with job security. White men will fill those slots. They want an outer core of easily dispensable manual and clerical workers. That's where women and blacks enter.

(David Thomas, 'The jobs bias against the blacks', in *New Society,* November 1984)

---

a) What does the data in Item A tell us about the jobs of women and members of ethnic minorities? (4 marks)

b) According to Item B, why has there been an increasing need for part-time workers? (3 marks)

c) Referring to Items B and C, explain why badly paid jobs are so often done by women. (6 marks)

d) Using the data here (and from elsewhere if you wish), explain the relationship between class, gender and ethnic stratification. (12 marks)

Question 6 **Age and Stratification**

United Kingdom	0—4	5—14	15—29	30—44	45—59	60—64	65—74	75—84	85+	Millions All Ages
Mid-year estimates										
1951	4.3	7.0	10.3	11.1	9.6	2.4	3.7	1.6	0.2	50.3
1961	4.3	8.1	10.3	10.5	10.6	2.8	4.0	1.9	0.3	52.8
1971	4.5	8.9	11.8	9.8	10.2	3.2	4.8	2.2	0.5	55.9
1981	3.5	8.1	12.8	11.0	9.5	2.9	5.2	2.7	0.6	56.4
1986	3.6	7.2	13.5	11.5	9.2	3.1	5.0	3.0	0.7	56.8
1987	3.7	7.1	13.5	11.6	9.2	3.0	5.0	3.0	0.8	56.9
Projections										
1991	3.9	7.1	12.9	12.1	9.5	2.9	5.0	3.1	0.9	57.5
1996	4.1	7.6	11.6	12.6	10.5	2.7	5.0	3.1	1.1	58.3
2001	3.9	8.1	10.8	13.2	11.0	2.8	4.8	3.2	1.2	59.0
2006	3.6	8.1	11.0	12.6	11.6	3.2	4.8	3.2	1.2	59.3
2011	3.5	7.5	11.7	11.3	12.1	3.7	5.2	3.1	1.3	59.4
2025	3.8	7.4	11.2	11.3	11.1	4.1	6.0	3.9	1.4	60.0

(*Social Trends 19*, HMSO, London, 1989)

ITEM B **RETIREMENT**

In the United States and the European countries where the work role is the chief determinant of status and where retirement is dictated by the calendar, the older retired person is left without valued roles to perform. To be sure they may keep busy gardening, babysitting, housekeeping, or fishing, but these activities are little valued in the society at large and are scarcely visible outside the immediate circle of the nuclear family.

(Donald Cowgill and Lowell Holmes, 'Ageing and modernisation', 1972, in Vida Carver (ed.), *An Ageing Population*, Hodder and Stoughton, London, 1978)

ITEM C **HYPOTHERMIA**

Even disregarding the problems of under-reporting, and difficulties with diagnosis, official statistics for Great Britain show that each year some 1,000 people die from conditions associated with hypothermia – low body temperature. The vast majority of these deaths occur among elderly people. This is bad enough, particularly when the individual tragedies behind the statistics are revealed – such as the 82 year-old man found dead during the last big freeze, huddled in front of a switched-off electric fire, or the 79-year-old woman who collapsed as, too late, she moved to turn on her single bar gas heater.

(Malcolm Wicks, 'Frozen in poverty', *The Guardian*, 21 November 1988)

ITEM D CHILDREN IN THE LABOUR MARKET

There is a huge, invisible workforce of children doing a vast range of jobs: paper rounds; milk deliveries; jobs in markets, restaurants, shops, farms, garages, factories. Indeed many small businesses depend on child labour. High levels of unemployment mean that a child may be the only breadwinner in a family. And, with increasing privatisation, companies offering the lowest tenders win contracts. Child employees will therefore be paid less so that the company can do the work cheaper.

Most children look on a casual job as a valuable asset – a source of independence, responsibility, financial freedom and work experience. For children, time spent in a part-time job could seem more important to their chances of future employment than school. For an employer, juvenile labour is cheap, dispensable and replaceable.

As employees, children have no rights over pay or dismissal. As illegal employees, they have no rights to insurance or compensation for injury. The school-age workforce rarely complains. They have few enough rights; they deserve one more – the right not to be exploited.

(Joanna Head, 'Children's hours', *New Society*, 26 February 1988)

---

a) Describe the changing age structure of the population as illustrated in Item A.   (5 marks)

b) With reference to Item B, explain what happens to a person's status as they become elderly and suggest why.   (4 marks)

c) What are the similarities in the status of children and the elderly? Illustrate your answer with evidence from Items C and D.   (4 marks)

d) With reference to any of the data here explain what problems a sociologist might have gathering reliable and representative data on the experiences of children and the elderly.   (5 marks)

e) Using data from here and elsewhere, explain why sociologists should take account of age when studying stratification.   (7 marks)

Question 7 **The Middle Class : 1**

ITEM A **DISTRIBUTION OF ECONOMICALLY ACTIVE POPULATION**

Great Britain   Percent

Standardized Census occupational category	1911 M	1911 F	1931 M	1931 F	1951 M	1951 F	1961 M	1961 F	1971 M	1971 F
Self-employed and higher-grade salaried professionals	1.5	1.0	1.7	1.0	2.8	1.0	4.5	1.1	6.1	1.4
Employers and proprietors	7.7	4.3	7.6	4.4	5.7	3.2	4.8	3.0	5.2	2.9
Administrators and managers	3.9	2.3	4.5	1.6	6.8	2.7	7.5	2.6	9.9	3.3
Lower-grade salaried professionals and technicians	1.4	5.8	1.8	6.0	3.0	7.9	4.0	9.2	5.5	10.8
Inspectors, supervisors, and foremen	1.8	0.2	2.0	0.4	3.3	1.1	3.8	0.9	4.5	1.2
Clerical workers	5.1	3.3	5.1	10.3	6.0	20.3	6.5	25.5	6.1	28.0
Sales personnel and shop assistants	5.0	6.4	5.9	8.2	4.0	9.6	3.9	10.0	3.9	9.4
Skilled manual workers (inc. self-employed artisans)	33.0	24.6	30.1	19.2	30.3	12.7	32.3	10.8	29.4	9.3
Semi-skilled manual workers	29.1	47.0	23.4	41.4	24.3	33.6	22.8	30.9	21.2	27.3
Unskilled manual workers	11.5	5.1	17.9	7.5	13.8	7.9	9.9	6.0	8.2	6.4
Total active population (Thousands)	12,926	5,424	14,760	6,263	15,584	6,930	15,992	7,649	15,609	8,762

(Adapted from A. H. Halsey, *Change in British Society*, Oxford University Press, Oxford, 1986)

ITEM B **A NEW MIDDLE CLASS**

The position of the white collar worker in the class structure has recently been exciting as much comment as the state of the working class. The proportion of white-collar employees in the working population is increasing and, in Britain, it is expected that, by the end of the century, the manual strata will be outnumbered. This has already happened in America. Hence the claim that advanced industrial societies are becoming increasingly middle class is not without some foundation. But what type of middle class is growing? Commentators have agreed that the middle class is changing. A generation ago, it was conventional to treat self-employed business men and professional people as archetypal (typical) middle class figures. Middle class values have traditionally emphasised the virtues of individual enterprise, the security that accompanies the possession of private property and the desirability of conserving one's assets along with the social arrangements that made their accumulation possible. Will the growth of the white-collar sector lead to the spread of these traditional middle class values or is a new middle class being shaped and, if so, what values will it nurture?

(K. Roberts et al, *The Fragmentary Class Structure*, Heinemann, London, 1977)

Great Britain

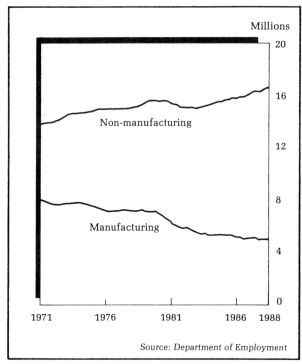

Source: Department of Employment

(*Social Trends 19*, HMSO, London, 1989)

a) Using Item A, identify the main changes that took place in the occupational structure of Great Britain between 1911 and 1971. (4 marks)

b) In which occupational category has female employment increased the most? Why has this happened? (6 marks)

c) Briefly state Roberts' main argument in Item B and choose four statistics from Item A which support it. (6 marks)

d) If the trend indicated by Item C continues, what are the likely consequences for employment, class structure and voting behaviour? (9 marks)

Question 8 **The Middle Class: 2**

ITEM A **WHITE COLLAR PROLETARIANS**

White-collar proletarians are not mythical creatures. There are thousands of them and they can be found in the exact circumstances that previous exponents of the proletarianisation thesis have identified. The proletarians in our non-manual sample were distinguished by their relatively depressed socio-economic conditions. They were typically employed in routine jobs at the base of the white-collar occupational hierarchy, income levels were below the average for other white-collar groups, and a relatively large proportion had received no post-secondary education whatsoever. Furthermore, levels of expressed job satisfaction were exceptionally low. **Proletarian outlooks** were common amongst individuals who had entered office jobs immediately upon leaving school, but had never obtained the further qualifications necessary to climb far up a career ladder.

The non-manual tasks that an office worker is required to perform need not be intellectually stimulating. Similarly, the opportunities that are available to exercise authority and assume responsibility in many 'salaried' occupations are minimal. Given such conditions, white-collar workers are liable to regard themselves as part of the working class.

(K. Roberts et al, *the Fragmentary Class Structure,* Heinemann, London, 1977)

ITEM B **TEACHER UNIONS**

The main teachers' unions held their annual conferences over Easter, and several modified their policies towards the government in several ways. For example, the National Union of Teachers, the largest union, voted against a policy of non-compliance with the new education act and established an 'Independent Education Commission' to monitor its introduction. This decision contrasts markedly with the NUT's recent, more combative responses to government policy.

. . . it is not for want of trying that teachers have never attained full professional standing. Parry and Parry (1974) suggest an explanation for this failure, and make a comparison with doctors. In the 19th century, both groups made efforts to improve their market situation. Teachers, assisted by the establishment of training colleges in the 1840s, set up the College of Preceptors in 1846, but its scope was limited.

Parry and Parry argue that, once the state adopted a major role in the provision of schooling from 1870 onwards, and became the main employer of teachers, it was against the state's interests to allow teachers the professional independence achieved by doctors.

In the Parrys' view, the state's success in preventing the professionalisation of teachers has been helped by the internal division of the occupation. It is divided by the status of subjects, by the age group of pupils, by gender differences, by religious differences, and by the existence of the private sector. In addition, teachers have not established an exclusive body of knowledge, as have doctors and lawyers.

(Pat McNeill, 'Teachers and unions', *New Society,* 29 April 1988)

ITEM C **SECRETARIAL WORK**

At one end of the scale is the pool typist. She works alongside other pool typists and her work consists wholly of copy typing, which has been given to her by a number of junior managers, or allocated to her by a pool supervisor. Her job is thus totally routine with immediate visible results which are easily measured. Her success is entirely dependent on her speed and accuracy of typing and thus communication with other people is not only unimportant but in most cases is disruptive to performance. Even work originators tend not to brief her personally on the typing; they will merely leave her some written instructions. The pool typist characterizes a secretarial position where activities are wholly mechanistic.

At the other end of the scale is the senior executive secretary or personal assistant to the managing director. She may spend little or no time typing since she may have her own junior secretary to whom such tasks can be delegated. Instead, most of her day is spent in a supportive administrative capacity carrying out a variety of tasks, from making the coffee to taking her boss's place at a meeting. This kind of secretary works very closely with her boss, and indeed, her success depends vitally on maintaining his coordinated team approach. The personal secretary not only undertakes anything required of her by her boss but also, and importantly, initiates many work-based activities herself.

(S. Vinnicombe, 'The secretarial role', in Eric Butterworth and David Weir (eds.), *The New Sociology of Modern Britain*, Fontana, London, 1984)

a) What is a 'white-collar proletarian' (Item A)? (2 marks)

b) Explain what is meant by the 'proletarian outlooks' mentioned in Item A. How might these affect the actions of office workers? (4 marks)

c) Explain the argument in Item B for seeing doctors but not teachers as professionals. (4 marks)

d) Suggest what evidence a sociologist might collect in order to test the hypothesis that clerical workers are proletarian. (6 marks)

e) Using the evidence here and from elsewhere assess the view that parts of the middle class are being 'proletarianised'. (9 marks)

Question 9 **The Working Class**

ITEM A **THE TRADITIONAL WORKING CLASS**

The salient (main) characteristics of the 'traditional' type of working class district could be said to derive from the relative stability and the social homogeneity of its population. The tightly knit network of kinship and the close ties of familiarity between neighbours are the products of successive generations of families living out their lives alongside each other; the strong sense of communal solidarity and the various forms of mutual help and collective action reflect the absence of any wide economic, cultural or status differences . . . the community constitutes a closely defined pattern for social living and one, moreover, which is highly resistant to change.

(J. H. Goldthorpe, D. Lockwood, et al., *The Affluent Worker in the Class Structure*, Cambridge University Press, Cambridge, 1968)

ITEM B USE OF 'LEISURE' TIME

COUPLE A   Migrated from Scotland seven years previously; husband a setter at Skefko; one daughter aged three; wife pregnant and not working; have recently bought a new semi-detached house.

	HUSBAND	WIFE
Week-day 1		
Evening	Worked on building a garage to adjoin house	Did housework
Week-day 2		
Evening	Fitted new cupboard and shelves in kitchen	Watched TV
Saturday		
Morning	[Worked overtime]	Went shopping in Luton with daughter
Afternoon	[Worked overtime]	Did housework
Evening	Drove to other side of Luton to collect cement for use on garage	Watched TV
Sunday		
Morning	[Worked overtime]	Did housework
Afternoon	Laid linoleum in kitchen	Played with daughter
Evening	Watched TV	Watched TV and knitted

COUPLE D   Have lived in Luton for seventeen years, originally from the Midlands; husband a process worker at Laporte on shiftwork; two teenage sons; wife works full-time at a dry cleaner's, also on shifts; now buying their own home.

	HUSBAND	WIFE
Week-day 1		
Afternoon	Helped elder son to paint his motor scooter	Did housework
Week-day 2		
Afternoon	Went shopping for provisions Worked on repairs to car	Did housework Watched TV
Saturday		
Morning	Did housework with wife	(see husband)
Afternoon	Went shopping in Luton with wife	(see husband)
Evening	Watched TV	Watched TV
Sunday		
Morning	Stayed in bed	Did housework
Afternon	Visited for lunch by a couple of 'old friends'	(see husband)
Evening	Watched TV	Went to bed early

(J. H. Goldthorpe, D. Lockwood, et al., *Op. Cit.*)

ITEM C NEW DIVISIONS

Lukes argues that technological change, the increased participation of women in paid labour . . . with the shift from manufacturing to service industries, have made the distinction between manual and non-manual labour largely irrelevant. Indeed, with the rise of mass production and consumption, labour or work itself has become less central to the identity and consciousness of workers. More and more, the working class is concerned with issues of consumption – of housing and of state benefit, for example. According to Lukes, recent research shows Britain to be a society divided against itself in new ways: those with a stake in private property and those without; those self-sufficient on wages versus welfare claimants; the populations of declining regions against those resident in economically buoyant areas; those in relatively secure occupational or company career-ladders against the unemployed and subemployed who are on the economic margins of society. These new sectional interests are reflected, it seems, in the growth of instrumental, pecuniary (money-orientated) egoistic (in short, capitalist) values and attitudes, and in a corresponding decline in older forms of solidarity based on community, unionism, or class itself. British workers, having come to terms with the acquisitive (valuing material possessions) society, have settled down in a mood of quiet disillusionment to seek their private satisfactions at home and in leisure and to pursue conflicting sectional demands in the workplace.

(Gordon Marshall, 'What is happening to the working class?', *Social Studies Review*, Vol. 2, No. 3, Jan 1987)

ITEM D VOTING INTENTIONS

			Service		SOCIAL CLASS Intermediate		(Goldthorpe) Working	
HOUSING TENURE/ VOTE	Owner-occupied	Conservative	51	(136)	49	(146)	25	(58)
		Labour	19	(51)	22	(64)	50	(113)
		Alliance	24	(63)	21	(63)	17	(39)
		Would not vote	6	(17)	8	(25)	8	(18)
	Local authority, rented	Conservative	17	(4)	22	(15)	15	(22)
		Labour	39	(9)	50	(34)	63	(90)
		Alliance	26	(6)	16	(11)	13	(18)
		Would not vote	17	(4)	12	(8)	9	(13)
	Privately rented	Conservative	50	(11)	39	(17)	34	(11)
		Labour	32	(7)	16	(7)	53	(17)
		Alliance	14	(3)	21	(9)	13	(4)
		Would not vote	5	(1)	25	(11)	0	(0)

Notes (i) Percentages may not add up to 100 because of rounding.
　　　 (ii) Figures in brackets are raw numbers.

(Gordon Marshall, *op. cit.*)

a) What is the likely affect on the traditional working class community (Item A) of the behaviour described in Item B? (6 marks)

b) Identify and explain factors from Item B which might explain why the behaviour of these couples does not conform to the accepted pattern of the traditional working class as implied by Item A. (7 marks)

c) Using Items C and D, assess the view that traditional class divisions have been replaced by new socio-economic divisions. (7 marks)

d) How might an awareness of gender and ethnic differences alter a sociological account of the working class today? (5 marks)

Question 10 **The Underclass**

COLONIAL IMMIGRANTS

What we set out to do in the empirical studies reported in this book was to discover something of the relationship between West Indian and Asian immigrants, and their children and the class structure (or class struggle) in British society. We wished to see how far they appeared, from what we could discover of their employment, housing and educational histories, to have attained the same position as other working-class people, and how far they identified with or participated in working-class organisations. The concept of underclass was intended to suggest the alternative possibility, namely that, instead of identifying with working class culture, community and politics, they formed their own organisations and became in effect a separate underprivileged class.

(J. Rex and S. Tomlinson, *Colonial Immigrants in a British City*, RKP, London, 1979)

ITEM B **UNDERCLASS: A USEFUL CONCEPT?**

We can see four arguments for using the term underclass, all of which differentiate blacks from the working class and therefore prevent them from being fully identified with it. Firstly, blacks are subject to racial discrimination and need to find ways of fighting it. Secondly, blacks as a group tend to be poorer than the working class as a whole: in that sense they are an 'underclass'. Thirdly, the trade union movement and, perhaps to a lesser extent, the Labour Party, has failed to adequately meet the needs of black people. Fourthly, blacks have produced their own cultural and, to some extent, political institutions, and it seems likely that these will be further developed. Self-help is, perhaps, the first and last line of preservation.

(Mike O'Donnell, *A New Introduction to Sociology*, 2nd Nelson, Walton-on-Thames, 1987)

ITEM C **A TEENAGE TRAP**

Chris from Birmingham is down on his luck. He pulls a few pounds from the pocket of his ripped leather jacket. That will tide him over till the end of the week; then he will be back on the scrounge. Two weeks ago he had his last remaining source of legitimate income cut off. Now he does his best to make ends meet from day to day. 'I don't think I can survive for long like this,' he says, adding nonchalantly: 'I suppose I'll have to think of something else.'

Chris does not look, talk or act like the stereotype of the wide-eyed and bushy-tailed 17-year-old. He left school two years ago and has been living off state benefits ever since. Though he would like a job, employers will not take him because they dislike his punky clothes and hair gelled into the shape of a trident.

Chris is just one of hundreds of teenagers in Birmingham, together with an estimated 90,000 nationally, trapped by new government benefits regulations. The Department of Social Security ruled in September that unemployed 16 and 17-year-olds would only be given money to live on if they enrolled on a government-sponsored Youth Training Scheme. Chris refused to join a YTS. He thinks that young people are being conned into working full-time for 'slave wages' – just £28 a week for most school-leavers. Having had his benefit cut off, he now ekes a precarious living through petty crime, begging and charity.

(Edward Pilkington, 'Caught in a teenage trap', *The Guardian,* November 23 1988)

ITEM D **COLLAPSE IN TRADITIONAL VALUES**

One of the most serious problems is a collapse in traditional values. Illegitimacy rates in the underclass have doubled in 20 years (USA figures). In some American cities, less than 25% of black children are born in homes with a father present. This has meant more than a decline in living standards. It has meant the loss of any sense of social authority among a generation. For these children, who have a seen a real drop in their standard of living of 25 per cent since 1977, failure rates at school are climbing. If the situation is to be saved, it has to be by reaching people whose closest idea of authority – a father – has never existed.

As if to compound this, drug use has been making dramatic gains in this group. Intra-venous needles have had the added effect of spreading AIDS, now an epidemic in America only among the underclass. The development of more addictive drugs, such as crack, has above all broken single mothers. The proportion of women addicts at a major New York treatment centre doubled with the arrival of the drug. Yet these mothers are the community's last defence against social catastrophe.

Tories, of all people, should understand that the underclass is not essentially an economic problem. It is a cultural problem. It demands cultural, not economic solutions: education and workfare[1] from government, and a greater sense of responsibility and self-criticism from the community itself. That, at least, is what the experience has taught. There is still time for Britain to learn from it.

(1) A form of compulsory work for the unemployed.

(Andrew Sullivan, 'The class below the bottom line', *The Daily Telegraph,* July 13, 1988)

a) With which sociological perspective do you associate the idea of an underclass? Give reasons for your answer. (4 marks)

b) With reference to Items A, B and D, consider how important ethnicity is to the study of stratification. (6 marks)

c) In Item C Chris is described as being caught in a 'Teenage Trap'. What is this trap and what prevents him from getting out of it? (4 marks)

d) What does Andrew Sullivan mean in Item D when he says that the underclass is a cultural not an economic problem? (5 marks)

e) What criticisms could be made of the analysis of, and the solutions for the underclass suggested by Sullivan in Item D? (6 marks)

5 Work and Leisure

Question 1 Ownership and Control in 'Capitalist' Society

ITEM A SHARE OWNERSHIP: PRIVATISED COMPANIES AND TSB

Individuals[1] by sex, age and social class, Great Britain, 1987

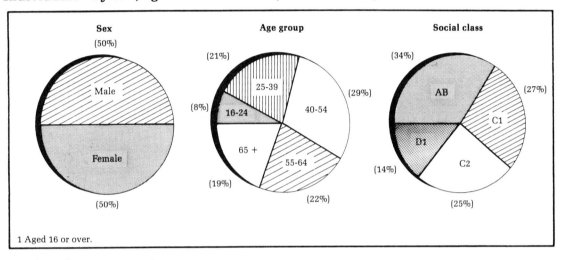

1 Aged 16 or over.

(*Social Trends 18*, HMSO, London, 1988)

ITEM B SHARE OWNERSHIP: BRITISH COMPANIES (1963-1970)

	% of shares held		
Category of owner	1963 (all cos.)	1969 (all cos.)	1975 (all cos.)
Persons, executors, trustees	54.0	47.4	42.1
Insurance companies	10.0	12.2	14.9
Pension funds	6.4	9.0	15.2
Investment trusts	7.4	7.6	4.7
Unit trusts	1.3	2.9	2.0
Banks	1.3	1.7	2.1
Stock exchange	1.4	1.4	0.1
Other financial cos.	2.6	1.1	0.5
Non-financial cos.	5.1	5.4	2.2
Public sector	1.5	2.6	0.8
Charities	2.1	2.1	4.2
Overseas	7.0	6.6	3.5
Totals	100.0	100.0	92.3

(Nicholas Abercrombie et al., *Contemporary British Society*, Polity Press, Cambridge, 1988)

ITEM C INDUSTRIAL AND CAPITALIST SOCIETY

In *Class and Class Conflict in Industrial Society (1959)*, Ralf Dahrendorf directly compares the relative usefulness of the concepts of **'industrial'** and **'capitalist'** society. While the latter was used by Marx, Dahrendorf makes a case for claiming that the former is to be preferred as a more inclusive term for understanding Western societies.

Capitalism, he says, is only one mode of organising an industrial society – a transitory form, limited to the Western European societies in the nineteenth and early twentieth centuries. A capitalist society, in his view, is one in which industrial production lies primarily in private hands: in which the industrial entrepreneur (or capitalist) is at once the owner of a factory or factories, and the chief directive authority over the workers. But with the increasing scale of industry since Marx's day, the ownership of capital no longer gives control over the enterprise. Those who control industrial production today, especially in the large firms which come increasingly to predominate in the economy, are managerial executives. Capitalist society has, therefore, been replaced by a new form of industrial society.

(Anthony Giddens, *Sociology: A Brief but Critical Introduction,* 2nd edition, Macmillan, Basingstoke, 1986)

ITEM D DIRECTORS AND SHAREHOLDERS

The majority of directors are indeed substantial shareholders and, therefore, have an additional source of income. While their percentage holding in any particular company may be very small, the monetary value of shares held is considerable and directors tend to hold shares in a wide range of companies. Top corporate 'management' and the large personal shareholders are one and the same group. The shareholdings of directors give them an interest in the success of the business system as a whole: their general financial interests are identical to those of the financial intermediaries, and their shareholdings are often managed on a day-to-day basis by bank investment departments.

(John Scott, 'Does Britain still have a ruling class?', *Social Studies Review,* Vol. 2, No. 1., 1986)

---

a) What do Items A and B tell us about the ownership of British companies?

(4 marks)

b) With reference to Item C explain what you understand by the terms 'capitalist' and 'industrial' society.

(4 marks)

c) Does the evidence in Items A and B support either the view that Britain is a capitalist or an industrial society? What additional information might a sociologist need about the ownership and control of industry to answer this question?

(7 marks)

d) Does John Scott's evidence in Item D support or contradict the idea that 'capitalist society has . . . been replaced by a new form of industrial society'?

(5 marks)

e) Explain what problems a sociologist might have researching the relationship between the ownership and control of industry.

(5 marks)

Question 2 **Alienation**

For Marx, alienation had four dimensions. First, workers in a capitalist society are divorced from the products of their labour. People put themselves into the goods they produce, but under capitalism the goods are then expropriated and sold for profit.

Second, the process of production becomes fragmented; labour becomes an uninteresting chore, meaningless, unfulfilling and unrewarding – a means to an end rather than an end in itself.

Third, at the social level people become alienated from others, as relationships come to be dominated by the market. Consequently the cooperative nature of human enterprise is corrupted.

Fourth, humans are alienated from their 'species being', for manual work is made mindless and uncreative. Capitalist production relations separate design and planning (mental labour) from routine manual labour, and reduces manual work to a bestial, inhuman level.

(Tony Bilton et al., *Introductory Sociology,* 2nd edition, Macmillan, Basingstoke, 1987)

ITEM B **ALIENATION TRENDS : THE LONG VIEW**

Alienation has travelled a course that could be charted on a graph by means of an inverted U-curve.

In the early period, dominated by craft industry, alienation is at its lowest level and the worker's freedom at a maximum. Freedom declines and the curve of alienation (particularly in its powerlessness dimension) rises sharply in the period of machine industry. The alienation curve continues upward to its highest point in the assembly-line industries of the twentieth century. In automotive production, the combination of technological, organisational, and economic factors has resulted in the simultaneous intensification of all dimensions of alienation.

But with automated industry there is a counter-trend, one that we can fortunately expect to become even more important in the future. The case of the continuous-process industries, particularly the chemical industry, show that automation increases the worker's control over his work process and checks the further division of labour and growth of large factories. The result is meaningful work in a more cohesive, integrated industrial climate. The alienation curve begins to decline from its previous height as employees in automated industries gain a new dignity from responsibility and a sense of individual function – thus the inverted U.

(R. Blauner, *Alienation and Freedom,* University of Chicago Press, Chicago, 1964)

ITEM C **FACTORY WORK**

The first day in a factory terrifies everyone, many people will speak to me about it later, often with anguish. What mind, what body can accept this form of slavery, this destructive rhythm of the assembly line, without some show of resistance? It's against nature. The aggressive wear and tear of the assembly line is experienced violently by everyone, city workers and peasants, intellectual and manual workers, immigrants and Frenchmen. And it's not unusual to see a new recruit give up after his first day, driven mad by the noise, the sparks, the inhuman pressure of speed, the harshness of endlessly repetitive work, the authoritarianism of the bosses and the severity of the orders, the dreary prison-like atmosphere which makes the shop so frigid. Months and years in there? How can one imagine such a thing? No: better escape, poverty, the insecurity of little odd jobs, anything!

Night. I can't sleep. As soon as I close my eyes I see piles of 2 CVs, a sinister procession of grey car bodies. I see again Sadok's porn magazine among the sandwiches and the oil drums and the metal. Everything's ugly. And those 2 CVs, that interminable string of 2 CVs ... The alarm clock goes off. Six o'clock already? I ache all over, I'm just as worn out as I was last evening. What have I done with my night?

(Robert Linhart, *The Assembly Line*, John Calder, London, 1981)

ITEM D ABSENTEEISM BY SECTOR

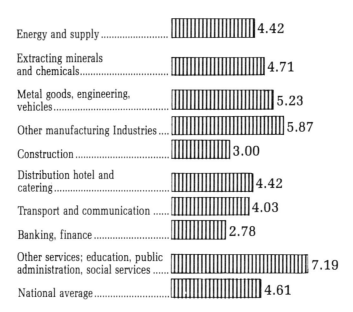

Percentage of working days lost in 1985

Energy and supply	4.42
Extracting minerals and chemicals	4.71
Metal goods, engineering, vehicles	5.23
Other manufacturing Industries	5.87
Construction	3.00
Distribution hotel and catering	4.42
Transport and communication	4.03
Banking, finance	2.78
Other services; education, public administration, social services	7.19
National average	4.61

In 1986 the management at the Vauxhall car plant at Luton cracked down on the problem of absenteeism at work. On Mondays and Fridays as many as one in five production workers was not bothering to turn up. The overall level of absenteeism was as high as 13 per cent. The problem was costing the company £7 million a year in lost production. For British industry as a whole, the problem cost 40 times more in lost production than strikes.

(Adapted from *The Guardian*, 1986)

a) What are the main differences between the views of Marx and Blauner on alienation, expressed in Items A and B? (6 marks)

b) In what ways might Marx and Blauner disagree about the long-term solution to the problem of alienation as described in Item C? (5 marks)

c) With reference to the concepts of 'job satisfaction' and 'alienation', together with any other relevant factors, explain the differences between the absenteeism of Vauxhall workers and those working in banking and finance described in Item D. (8 marks)

d) How might sociologists research alienation and what problems might they face? (6 marks)

Question 3 **Industrial Conflict**

ITEM A UNION MEMBERS, EARNINGS, STRIKES, UNEMPLOYMENT

	Union members (000)	Density (%)	Change in real earnings (%)	Strikes	Striker–days (000)	Registered unemployment (%)
1978	13112	54.1	+ 4.6	2498	9405	5.7
1979	13289	54.4	+ 2.0	2125	29474	5.3
1980	12947	52.6	+ 3.8	1348	11964	6.8
1981	12106	49.3	− 0.7	1344	4266	10.4
1982	11593	48.0	+ 2.3	1538	5313	12.1
1983	11236	46.8	+ 2.5	1364	3754	12.9
1984	10994	45.4	+ 1.9	1221	27135	13.1
1985	10716	43.3	+ 3.0	903	6402	13.5
1986	10333	41.6	+ 3.4	1074	1920	11.7 [1]
1987	10200	41.1	+ 4.8	1016	3546	10.7

(1) Change in Method of compilation explains 1985-86 decline

(Richard Hyman, 'What's happening to the unions?', *Social Studies Review,* Vol. 4, no. 4, March, 1989)

ITEM B TRADE UNION MEMBERSHIP BY GENDER AND AGE, 1983

	% who are trade union members		
	Males	Females	
Age	Full-time	Full-time	Part-time
16-19	21	24	5
20-4	47	45	21
25-34	56	52	29
35-44	59	56	33
45-64	67	58	38
65+	4	3	8
Total	57	50	33

(*General Household Survey 13,* HMSO, London, 1983)

There is a possibility that University lecturers who refuse to set or mark examination papers will be sent home and locked out, with the consequence that some Universities may shut down.

The boycott, organised by the Association of University Teachers after employers refused to make a pay offer, will affect thousands of students.

The Committee of Vice-Chancellors and Principals considered three options: to deduct pay from participating academics; to send home staff without pay; or summary dismissal.

The AUT, which is seeking a pay rise back-dated to April 1988, expressed 'incredulity and horror' at possible lock-outs. 'If vice-chancellors are to send staff home, the university management will prevent teaching, will stop education, and will cause immediate and irreparable damage to teaching programmes and to all students.

This movement will be sheer madness. We will be on a collision course.'

(Adapted from *The Independent*, 29 March, 1989)

ITEM D **INDUSTRIAL SABOTAGE**

They had to throw away half a mile of Blackpool rock last year, for, instead of the customary motif running through its length, it carried the terse injunction 'F_____ Off'. A worker dismissed by a sweet factory had effectively demonstrated his annoyance by sabotaging the product of his labour. In the Christmas rush in a Knightsbridge store, the machine which shuttled change backwards and forwards suddenly ground to a halt. A frustrated salesman had demobilized it by ramming a cream bun down its gullet. In our researches we have been told by Woolworth's sales girls how they clank half a dozen buttons on the till simultaneously to win a few minutes' rest from 'ringing up'. Railwaymen have described how they block lines with trucks to delay shunting operations for a few hours. Materials are hidden in factories, conveyor belts jammed with sticks, cogs stopped with wire and ropes, lorries 'accidentally' backed into ditches. Electricians labour to put in weak fuses, textile workers 'knife' through carpets and farmworkers cooperate to choke agricultural machinery with tree branches.

(L. Taylor and P. Walton, 'Industrial sabotage: motives and meanings', in S. Cohen (ed.). *Images of Deviance*, Penguin, Harmondsworth, 1971)

---

a) What are the main trends indicated by the statistics in Item A? (5 marks)

b) What do the figures in Item B tell us about trade union membership? (4 marks)

c) Using the data here and from elsewhere, suggest explanations for the trends indicated in Item A. (9 marks)

d) With reference to Items C and D comment on the validity of strike statistics, such as those in Item A, as accurate measures of industrial conflict. (7 marks)

Question 4 **Leisure and Social Class**

ITEM A PARTICIPATION IN SELECTED SPORTING ACTIVITIES

By socio-economic group, 1983

Great Britain	Percentages and numbers					
	Profess-ional, employers, and managers	Inter-mediate and junior non-manual	Skilled manual and own account non-prof-essional	Semi-skilled and unskilled manual	Full-time students	All persons
Percentage in each group engaging in each activity in the 4 weeks before interview						
Swimming, public outdoor pools	1	1	1	–	2	1
Swimming, other outdoor	5	4	3	2	6	3
Swimming indoor	9	10	5	4	17	7
Fishing	2	1	4	2	4	2
Sailing	1	–	–	–	1	–
Football	3	2	4	1	10	3
Rugby	1	–	–	–	3	–
Golf	7	2	2	1	3	2
Cricket	1	–	1	–	2	1
Tennis	2	2	1	–	6	1
Athletics, outdoor (field and track)	3	2	2	1	8	2
Keep fit/yoga	2	6	1	2	2	3
Gymnastics/athletics, indoor	1	1	1	1	3	1
Badminton	4	3	1	1	10	2
Squash	6	3	2	1	8	3
Table tennis	2	1	1	1	9	1
Darts	6	5	10	7	12	7
Billiards/snooker	9	5	13	6	18	8
Ten-pin bowling/bowls, indoor	1	1	1	1	1	1
Horse riding	1	1	–	–	3	1
Rambling, hiking	1	1	–	–	1	1
Walking (2 miles or more)	24	23	16	14	18	18
Cycling	2	2	1	1	6	2
Sample size (= 100%) (numbers)	2,390	5,628	4,108	5,653	550	19,050

(Social Trends 17, HMSO, London, 1987)

ITEM B A LEISURE-CENTRED CULTURE?

Stanley Parker, who has done much modern research into leisure, has said that 'today vestiges of the Protestant work ethic remain, but it has been strongly challenged by a more leisure-based ethic: that work is a means to the end of enjoying oneself in leisure. Earlier, work gave a man his sense of identity. Today, it is claimed, his leisure is more likely to supply it.' The extent to which we in Britain are in such a leisure-centred culture is debatable. We still rely on inherited attitudes. But soon the debate about whether or not we become more leisure-centred will be more urgent.

(Michael Williams, Society Today, Macmillan, Basingstoke, 1986)

ITEM C THE PREOCCUPATION OF THE ALLOTMENT

Peter Wright relates this preoccupation with the traditional working lives of County Durham: 'If he works with coal or metal or any other hard unyielding matter, his hobby will probably be keeping some form of livestock. On a nearby allotment, or at the bottom of his back garden, he will spend hours by his crudely built homemade pigeon cree, rattling a tin of corn and waiting in breathless excitement for his racing pigeons to come down, so that he can receive their rings and clock them in, hoping to win a prize. Or perhaps it is rabbits, their wet noses twitching against the rough, wire-fronted hutches that he is studying, show schedule in hand, trying to outpoint his rivals down the hill.'

Of course, the allotment was the ideal means of enjoying such pursuits. Separated from the home, it provided for a greater isolation and concentration, supportive of the intense competition but also the comradeship that surounds pigeon-keeping. It is frequently undertaken in pairs, two men sharing the experience, perhaps sharing the jobs on the allotment – one the vegetables, one the birds. Sometimes this is a purely pigeon partnership, and some have become renowned. In many of the pit villages, the duality of the pigeons and the vegetables provides the daily activity for the redundant miners.

(D. Crouch and C. Ward, *The Allotment*, Faber and Faber, London, 1988)

ITEM D FISHING

Down by the reservoir, the men crowd the trampled places between the reeds, flinging out their floats onto the rippling water. Hawthorn and elder bushes in acrid flower provide some screen from the noise and fumes of the busy motorway nearby.

This is where Mike comes in the evenings. He sits on what he regards as his own little promontory of dry earth, watching the insects skim over the water, and the gold stain of a smudged sun on the surface. His eight-year-old daughter, Katie, is content to sit beside him, drawing shapes in the well-trodden earth with a sharp stone. Suddenly, his rod jerks, Mike pulls vigorously, and a tench of about 1½ pounds leaps from the water.

'Fishing calms you. It's cheap once you have a rod. It's like everything else, you can buy all the fancy equipment, but I don't know that you get any more pleasure out of it for all that. Some of the animal liberation people tell you it's a cruel sport. I think they're wrong. You always throw back what you catch – a few poor buggers who've got nothing else might cook them and eat them, but they're very insipid. The only expense is the maggots – £1.20 a pint. Fishing is the biggest pastime in Britain. It relaxes people. If you take fishing away from the unemployed, you will have riots in the street.'

(Jeremy Seabrook, *The Leisure Society*, Blackwell, Oxford, 1988)

---

a) To what extent do the figures in Item A indicate a relationship between class and leisure? Explain your answer. (6 marks)

b) Briefly suggest sociological explanations for class differences among participants in darts and golf. (5 marks)

c) How might the miners' preoccupation with pigeons and allotments, described in Item C, be explained? (5 marks)

d) With reference to the evidence here, assess any one sociological theory of leisure. (9 marks)

Question 5 **Leisure and Gender**

ITEM A LEISURE TIME IN A TYPICAL WEEK, 1986

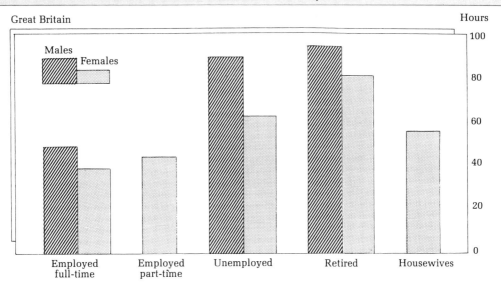

(*Social Trends 18*, HMSO, London, 1988)

ITEM B LEISURE ACTIVITIES BY GENDER

Per cent aged 16 or over engaging in each activity in the four weeks before the interview:

	males	females		males	females
Entertainment social and cultural activites			**Home-based activities**		
Going to the cinema	7	8	Listening to records/tapes	65	62
Visiting historic buildings	8	8	Gardening	50	39
Going to the theatre/ opera/ballet	4	5	Needlework/knitting	2	48
Going to museum/art galleries	3	3	House repairs/DIY	51	24
Amateur music/drama	3	3	Reading books	50	61
Attending leisure classes	1	2			
Going to fairs/amusement arcades	1	2			
Going out for a meal	41	40			
Going out for a drink	64	46			
Dancing	10	12			

(*General Household Survey 13*, HMSO, London, 1983)

ITEM C TIME FOR LEISURE

Finally, we have 'leisure' – with a mental sigh of relief. He's been to work, done the overtime, eaten and eliminated, taken the wife and kids for a run, and now at last he's free. To do what? Parker says: 'Leisure is time free from obligations either to self or to others – time in which to do as one chooses'. This is the place for enlarging the mind, doing one's hobbies, becoming a full human being, and so on. The problem for women is that they have very little of this time. So little, in fact, that it may become a threat when it exists, pointing up in relief the *lack* of autonomy and time for herself in the rest of her life. It is to be free from obligations – so no kids or grannies to look after. It is 'time in which to do as one chooses'. Anything at all? Take a day off for a walk? (What about the meals? Kids after school?) Go for a drink on your own in the evening? (What about the money? What about women alone in pubs? What about your husband's attitude to your mixing with other men?) Take a couple of hours off at lunchtime for a swim? (Who'll take care of the kids? How to stop thinking about your 'obligations' in so short a space of time?) The facilities don't exist for women's leisure: the creches, the proximity to home, the cheap entry fees.

(Sue McIntosh, 'A feminist critique of Stanley Parker's theory of work and leisure', in M. O'Donnell (ed.) *New Introductory Reader in Sociology,* Harrap, London, 1983)

ITEM D **SPORT FOR WOMEN**

Sport, like leisure, has always been male-defined, for men and by men, and it is supported not only by the structures and ideologies of male power within sport itself, but also by patriarchal relations in the household, community and economy. Women can be encouraged, subject to all kinds of caveats to do with class and ethnicity, to take up sport by involving existing non-sporting organizations, (women's organizations, playgroups etc.) or using places where women already go for other reasons (health centres, schools) and by providing things not previously provided, like low fees or a creche. But they will not remain in sport, or see it as an important part of their leisure, unless men's attitudes to women in sport and the home change and unless women can begin to permeate the power and decision making spheres of sport. But this is unlikely to happen without a major struggle, because the sporting activities of many men depend on the services provided by women (from cooking Sunday lunch so a morning male football match is able to go ahead unfettered by domestic responsibilities, to washing sports kit and giving verbal and emotional encouragement to sportsmen). If women start to see sport as something which does not largely exclude them, then men will find it more difficult to get the same levels of support they have previously enjoyed.

(Rosemary Deem, *All Work and No Play?,* Open University Press, Milton Keynes, 1986)

a) What conclusions can you draw from the data in Item A about the relationship between leisure and gender?   (4 marks)

b) Select from Item B leisure activities with significant differences in participation by sex. Suggest reasons for these differences.   (6 marks)

c) What criticisms could be made of Item B as sociological evidence?   (5 marks)

d) Using Items C and D, and from elsewhere if necessary, assess the view that leisure is primarily a male activity.   (10 marks)

Question 6 **Technological changes**

ITEM A **NEW TECHNOLOGY AT THE TIMES**

I don't think there is any dispute between management and unions, certainly not in Times Newspapers, about the physical improvement that new technology can bring to the working environment. The company now proposes to do away with its two hot metal composing rooms, one each for the *Times* and the *Sunday Times,* in which men have worked in the past on stone floors with machines, virtually the same as they were when they were first introduced 100 years ago. In their place will be a single composing room, cleaner, carpeted, even-temperatured, quieter, more attractively furnished, in which the new technology will be operated at the usual visual display units. No more metal to be melted on open pots; no more ink staining your hands, your clothes and getting down your fingernails; no more cleaning chemicals squirted around the room, and rags to be sent off to industrial cleaners; no more forms made of heavy metal in which the compositor can trap his fingers quite easily.

Only the most blinkered union militant would try to pretend that the new technology is anything but a vast improvement as far as the physical working conditions are concerned. Because the new process is also so much faster than the old, whoever works it (3000 lines of newspaper type per minute from a computerised phototypesetter compared with seven or eight lines per minute from the old Linotype machine) with keyboards which approximately double the rate of input, few employees are going to be required to complete the same workload. The result is that in the composing room, as opposed to the Company as a whole, Times Newspapers has proposed a reduction of between 40 and 45% of its workforce.

(Peter Harland of *The Times,* speaking at a conference in London, 1979)

ITEM B **NEW TECHNOLOGY AND ENGINEERING**

In my research, I investigated the introduction of micro-electronically controlled machines in engineering firms involved in what is called batch production. In this, goods are made not in continuous runs but in bursts of, for instance, 20 components at a time.

In one case study, an engineering company decided to automate a plating line. In plating, components are dropped into various solutions to coat them with a metal such as zinc or aluminium, Under the company's old system, three men worked each plating line. The men loaded parts onto a system of fixtures and controlled the fixtures as they dipped the parts into vats of different solutions. The workers also unloaded the 'plated' components at the end of the process.

In the new system, an electronic device controls the mechanisms holding the parts. The only jobs left (besides that of setting the equipment) are loading and unloading. So the new lines would each need only two workers, the increase in productivity paying for the new control system within a couple of years.

In terms of the conventional wisdom, the motivation for the new technology appear uncomplicated – improved production and so on. Yet during interviews with managers involved, I found that other factors were at work. **The managers complained that the workers were lazy and unreliable.** They would take long breaks, and would sometimes work slowly, leaving components in vats for longer than necessary.

In the eyes of the supervisors, 'automation' was a way of gaining greater control over the pace and quality of output. Further, managers tried to consolidate their new powers by putting the new controls well beyond the reach of any shop-floor worker – on the other side of the factory, where only managers and engineers were permitted.

(Barry Wilkinson, 'Battling I.T. out on the factory floor', *New Scientist,* 9 December, 1982)

ITEM C DIVISION OF LABOUR AND DESKILLING

In recent years, the division of labour and the deskilling of work have extended to many more occupations, aided very often by the computer. Mike Cooley describes how the engineering draughtsman in the 1930s was at the centre of design work in industry. 'He could design a component, draw it, stress it out, specify the material for it and the lubrication required.' Nowadays the work is divided between several specialists: the 'draughtsman draws, the metallurgist specifies the material, the stress analyst analyses the structure and the tribologist specifies the lubrication'.

The process of deskilling has been taken much further recently, however. A computer can now generate the drawings on which many draughtsmen would once have had to work, and the designer himself, using a VDU as an electronic drawing board, can produce drawings and detailed designs much faster. But even the professional in charge of a computer design facility may find his work partly deskilled as systematized design procedures are programmed into the computer to form what Cooley calls an 'automated design manual'. Thus the work of the designer has been undergoing exactly the same process of deskilling as manual work. Sometimes he is reduced to making a series of routine choices between fixed alternatives, in which case 'his skill as a designer is not used, and decays'.

(Arnold Pacey, *The Culture of Technology,* Blackwell, Oxford, 1983)

a) With reference to Item A explain why you think the unions opposed the introduction of new technology. (5 marks)

b) What different explanations can be suggested for the introduction of new technology at The Times? Use Items A and B in your answer. (7 marks)

c) In Item B, the 'managers complained that the workers were lazy and unreliable'. Suggest a variety of reason why this was so. (5 marks)

d) With reference to Item C and evidence from elsewhere describe and assess the Marxist argument that the new technology 'deskills' the workforce. (8 marks)

Question 7 **Unemployment**

Unemployment rates, seasonally adjusted (per cent)

FF

	1980	1981	1982	1983	1984	1985	1986	1987	1988
United Kingdom	5.1	8.1	9.5	10.5	10.7	10.9	11.1	10.0	8.0
North	8.0	11.8	13.3	14.6	15.3	15.4	15.2	14.0	11.9
Yorkshire & Humberside	5.3	8.9	10.4	11.4	11.7	12.0	12.4	11.3	9.5
East Midlands	4.5	7.4	8.4	9.5	9.8	9.9	9.9	9.0	7.2
East Anglia	3.8	6.3	7.4	8.0	7.9	8.0	8.1	6.8	4.8
South East	3.1	5.5	6.7	7.5	7.9	8.0	8.2	7.1	5.2
South West	4.5	6.8	7.8	8.7	9.0	9.3	9.5	8.2	6.3
West Midlands	5.5	10.0	11.9	12.9	12.7	12.7	12.6	11.1	8.5
North West	6.5	10.2	12.1	13.4	13.6	13.8	13.9	12.7	10.7
England	4.7	7.7	9.1	10.0	10.2	10.4	10.5	9.3	7.5
Wales	6.9	10.5	12.1	12.9	13.2	13.8	13.9	12.5	10.5
Scotland	7.0	9.9	11.3	12.3	12.6	12.9	13.3	13.0	11.2
Northern Ireland	9.4	12.7	14.4	15.5	15.9	16.1	17.6	17.6	16.4

(Regional Trends 24, HMSO, London, 1989)

Great Britain		Percentages and thousands		
			Women	
	Men	Married	Non-Married	All persons
Percentage of unemployed who left last job in previous 3 years because:				
Made redundant	40	14	26	32
Temporary job ended	23	17	23	22
Resigned	10	10	15	11
Family/personal	4	40	14	14
Health reasons	5	7	8	6
Retired	4	–	–	3
Other reasons/not stated	13	11	13	13
Total unemployed who left last job in previous 3 years (Thousands) (= 100%)	1,053	409	262	1,724
As percentage of all unemployed (percentages)	61	61	53	60

(Social Trends 19, HMSO, London, 1989)

ITEM C RECENT CHANGES IN CLASSIFYING UNEMPLOYMENT

Date	Change	Estimated effect on monthly count
Oct 1982	From a count of those registered for work at Jobcentres to a count of all benefit claimants.	−170,000 to −190,000
Apr 1983	Some men aged 60+ excluded from figures	−107,400
Jun 1983	Remaining men aged over 60 excluded	−54,000
Jun 1983	School leavers debarred from benefit until September each year	−100,000 to −200,000 (June to August)
Oct 1984	Change in eligibility to Community Programme	−29,000
Mar 1986	New 2-week delay in publication of monthly unemployment stats	average −50,000
Jun 1986	Change in method of counting unemployment using larger denominator	average −1.4%
Oct 1986	Some claimants with few National Insurance payments lose right to claim benefit	−24,000 after one year.
Oct 1986	Tighter availability for work test	−95,000 after one year.

(Adapted from David Taylor, 'Living with unemployment', Alan and Carol Walker (eds.), *The Growing Divide*, CPAG, London, 1987)

ITEM D FEMALE UNEMPLOYMENT

Women who have paid jobs are concentrated disproportionately in the public sector. They comprise 41 per cent of the total labour force, but 47 per cent of public sector employees (including 78 per cent of NHS and 86 per cent of local authority health and personal social services employees). This concentration makes women's jobs immediately and directly vulnerable to cuts in public spending. In addition, the number of employees in private sector service industries, in which women are also concentrated, fell slightly between 1979 and 1983.

Overall, between 1979 and 1986 male unemployment rose by 143 per cent, from 887,200 to 2,159,600; during the same period female unemployment rose by 189 per cent, from 346,700 to 1,001,700. Until 1983 both male and female unemployment grew rapidly; since then male unemployment has levelled off and fallen slightly, but unemployment has continued to rise among women. The continued rise in women's unemployment has, ironically, happened in spite of the fact that the November 1982 change in the method of calculating unemployment figures actually increased the invisibility of women's unemployment.

(Caroline Glendenning, 'Impoverishing women', in Alan and Carol Walker, *op. cit.*)

a) Describe the main trends in unemployment as illustrated in Item A. (4 marks)

b) What conclusions about unemployment and gender do you draw from Item B? (4 marks)

c) Choose any one change in the measurement of unemployment and explain why it would affect unemployment statistics. (3 marks)

d) Why is measuring female unemployment particularly difficult? Use data from here and elsewhere in your answer. (7 marks)

e) Discuss the view that 'no government agency in the world produces totally sociologically satisfactory unemployment statistics' (John Horne). (7 marks)

Question 8 **The 'Black' Economy**

ITEM A **THE INFORMAL ECONOMY**

We are using the term *informal economy* to cover the following three areas, of which the first two are the most important for our argument:

1. *Household economy:* production, not for money, by members of a household and predominantly for members of that houshold, of goods or services for which approximate substitutes might otherwise be purchased for money.

2. *Underground, hidden* or *black economy:* production, wholly or partly for money or barter, which should be declared to some official taxation or regulatory authority, but which is wholly or partly concealed.

3. *Communal economy:* production, not for money or barter, by an individual or group, of a commodity that might otherwise be purchaseable, and of which the producers are not principal consumers.

(J. I. Gershuny and R. E. Pahl, 'Britain in the decade of the three economies', in M. O'Donnell, *New Introductory Reader in Sociology,* Harrap, London, 1983)

ITEM B **THE THREE ECONOMIES**

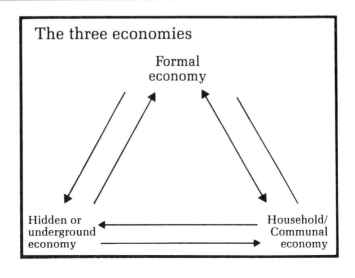

The diagram shows that, instead of a steady one-way flow of economic activity – whereby things move, over time, from the household to the industrial production system – there is a whole series of little transformations of production (perhaps taking place simultaneously) between the formal economy, the household economy and the under-ground economy. The direction of flow is determined by the social and technical conditions for the production of particular commodities at particular times. As the diagram shows, this involves six possible flows among three types of economy.

Here are some examples. The washing of clothes and linen, which moved from the wash house at home into the laundry, and then back into the home with the technological help of a washing machine, illustrates the two-way flow between households and the formal economy (1 and 2 in the diagram). The current prevalence of household construction work paid for in cash may indicate a shift from formal to underground, or 'black', production (3 in the diagram). And if unemployment levels rise, the cost of black work will drop and some jobs, now DIY, will move across (6).

(J. I. Gershuny and R. E. Pahl, *op. cit.*)

ITEM C A LABOUR MARKET?

We have come a long way from the classical Marxist labour force consisting simply of those who are regularly employed and others in various forms of the reserve army. The nature of wage-labour and unemployment has undergone some fundamental changes. The combined effect of expanded precarious work in regular jobs, wider use of government benefits, hustling, and the underground economy add up to something that looks very different from the traditional labor market. To the extent that capital uses the new arrangements to increase the degree of exploitation, the new situation is simply an erosion of the power of the workers. But insofar as people are able to turn the new forms of income-generating activity to their advantage, the structure is less of a **market** and more of a **terrain** in the struggle for some measure of social autonomy.

(P. Mattera, 'Off the books: the rise of the underground economy,' in John Horne, *Work and Unemployment,* Longman, Harlow, 1987)

ITEM D ALTERNATIVE ENTERTAINMENT

A combination of black DJs, illicit boot-leggers and pirate radio people have established an alternative entertainment sphere. This new environment started to shape itself in 1986 when white organisers of illegal warehouse parties began to work together with black sound systems like Soul II Soul. What warehouse parties started, pirate radio helps maintain. On London's 30 odd illegal radio stations, black music provides the main format.

Black Londoners who work for the pirates take pride in exercising an expertise excluded from the capital's entertainment mainstream. LWR London jock Steve Edwards : 'British legal radio is too controlled, too conservative. And its DJs are so complacent! We're not afraid to play our music'. The pirates have also discovered how to support themselves financially with advertising for gigs, shops and new record releases.

(Cynthia Rose, 'Thriving by night', *New Statesman and Society,* 17, June, 1988)

a) The diagram in Item B is explained with the help of two examples (washing clothes and household construction work). Choose two further examples and explain how they might move between the three economies. (6 marks)

b) Using the definition of the 'black economy' in Item A, suggest how a sociologist might research this activity and identify the problems that might be encountered. (6 marks)

c) Referring to Item C, explain why some see the growth of the 'black economy' as evidence of continued capitalist exploitation of the workforce, while others see it as evidence of resistance to that exploitation by the workforce. (5 marks)

d) Why has the 'black economy' become more significant in Britain recently? Refer to Item D and evidence from elsewhere in your answer. (8 marks)

Question 9 **Women and Waged Work**

ITEM A **THE RESERVE ARMY OF LABOUR?**

The Labour force is differentiated by gender, race and age. Those seeking labour are aware of these differences and may under certain economic conditions seek to exploit them. Disadvantaged groups may be much more likely to end up in secondary employment conditions, particuarly if they are women or members of ethnic minorities. This has sometimes been explained by a theory known as the **'reserve army of labour'.** This theory argues that, given the tendency for economic conditions to change (from recession to boom, for example), employers may use those who for various reasons are not permanently in a job (women with small children, the unemployed) when they need more workers. When production drops again or the boom ends, they can then dispose of the temporary workers fairy easily. The difficulty with this theory is that it does not explain very well the contemporary patterns of employment for groups like women, in particular the fact they rarely do, even on a temporary basis, the same jobs as men.

(Adapted from Rosemary Deem, *Work, Unemployment and Leisure*, Routledge, London, 1988)

Total, full-time and part-time participation rates: United Kingdom, 1984.

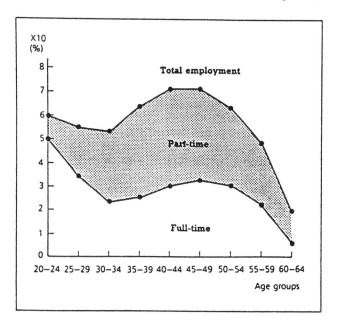

(A. Dale and J. Glover, 'Women's work patterns in the UK, France and the USA', in *Social Studies Review*, Vol. 3, No. 1, 1987).

ITEM C **EQUALITY OF JOB OPPORTUNITY**

The government is increasingly worried about the potential shortfall of young males in the workforce for the coming decade. So at last equality of job opportunity is being taken seriously. Demands are now being made for greater investment in the skills of women.

This is reflected in women's pay, which, according to the British Institute of Mangement, is rising more rapidly than men's.

Recent government legislation aims to prevent industry hindering the progress of women which is taken as evidence of its commitment to women.

Norman Fowler, the employment secretary, comments: 'In the 1990s, women will be playing a more and more important part in the labour market. It is vital to provide genuine equality of opportunity. Sex discrimination is not only unfair but harms the economy. Jobs should go to the best people, irrespective of sex.'

(Adapted from *The Sunday Times*, 29, January, 1989)

a) Referring to Item A explain what is meant by the 'reserve army of labour'. (2 marks)

b) Briefly explain why women are more likely to be in the 'reserve army of labour' than men. (5 marks)

c) Describe the pattern of female employment illustrated in Item B. (6 marks)

d) How would you account for the high rates of part-time work among women as illustrated in Item B? (2 marks)

e) To what extent is it true that women are in a separate labour market from men? In your answer comment on the view in Item C that 'at last equality of job opportunity is being taken seriously'. (10 marks)

Question 10 **Work and Ethnicity**

ITEM A **SOCIO-ECONOMIC CATEGORY BY ETHNIC GROUP**

Per cent

Job level	White	West Indian	Asian	Indian	Paki-stani	Bangla-deshi	African Asian	Muslim	Hindu	Sikh
Professional employer, management	19	5	13	11	10	10	22	11	20	4
Other non-manual	23	10	13	13	8	7	21	8	26	8
Skilled manual and foreman	42	48	33	34	39	13	31	33	20	48
Semi-skilled manual	13	26	34	36	35	57	22	39	28	33
Unskilled manual	3	9	6	5	8	12	3	8	3	6

(Nicholas Abercrombie et al., *Contemporary British Society*, Polity Press, Oxford, 1988)

ITEM B INDUSTRIAL SECTOR BY ETHNIC GROUP

	White	West Indian	Asian
			Per cent
Mining, chemicals and metal manufacture	9	4	7
Engineering and metals	15	9	13
Vehicles and ship-building	5	12	11
Textiles, clothing and leather	2	3	13
All other manufacturing	10	14	14
All manufacturing and mining industries	41	41	57
Construction	8	7	3
Transport and communication	10	24	12
Distributive trades	8	6	6
All other service industries	23	14	17
All service industries	41	45	35
Public administration defence	7	3	2

(Nicholas Abercrombie et al., *op. cit.*)

ITEM C IMMIGRANT LABOUR

After the second world war, people were encouraged to come to work in Britain in order to help overcome a severe labour shortage. Organisations such as London Transport and the National Health Service actively recruited people from the Caribbean who were prepared to do jobs that other people found undesirable.

Although the immigration of workers was severely curtailed after 1965, the characteristics of the black labour force today still reflect this migration of a generation ago. Black workers are still concentrated in unskilled and semi-skilled jobs which the population at large is reluctant to do. They still earn on average less than white people doing the same jobs, and are still more likely to be unemployed.

It might have been argued in the 1940s and 1950s that 'newcomers' should be happy at first to do unattractive work with low pay and bad conditions (which may still have been more attractive than what was available in their home country). But today, when half the black population were born and educated in Britain, the low aspirations of immigrants can no longer be used to explain the position of blacks in the labour market. Evidence shows that it is largely the result of racial discrimination.

(New Internationalist)

ITEM D THE JOBS BIAS AGAINST BLACKS

No one knows how many black teachers there are. Carlton Duncan – a Bradford headmaster and the only black secondary school head outside London – reckons most are in the bottom grades or supply teachers. In the West Indies, teaching was esteemed and a way to climb the social ladder. But Duncan says: 'I know black people who are discouraging their youngsters from going into the profession because of the lack of promotion and the racism.'

Even if no one knows how many black people work in the health service, we do know black doctors predominate in the unfashionable specialities of geriatrics and mental health. Among nurses, few blacks get senior jobs. The NHS has many black cleaners and canteen workers, but few black administrative and clerical staff. The ambulance service seems to be a 'no go' area.

It is the same in local governement. Researchers say that long-standing ethnic communities in cities like Birmingham and Cardiff are grossly under-represented in their local authority workforce. Liverpool city council, responsible for a black population estimated at 7.6 per cent, had 0.9 per cent black employees in 1982. The Greater London Council (abolished in 1986) now monitors the ethnic make-up of its workers, so we know that it has 15 black senior officers out of 553, six black craft supervisors out of 132, and 50 black firemen out of 6,951.

A monitoring exercise found that 0.9 per cent of civil servants in the north west and in Avon were black, way below the local ethnic population.

(David Thomas, 'The jobs bias against blacks', *New Society,* 1 November 1984)

ITEM E THE DUAL LABOUR MARKET

New job trends will work against black people. Research at the Institute of Manpower Studies at Sussex University suggests that companies are moving to a 'dual market' jobs policy. They want an inner core of highly paid professionals with job security. White men will fill those slots. They want an outer core of easily dispensable manual and clerical workers. That's where women and blacks enter.

(David Thomas, *op. cit.*)

---

a) What are the main differences between White, West Indian and Asian employment as shown in Item A?   (5 marks)

b) Select from Item B industrial sectors where White, West Indian and Asian workers seem to be over-represented. Briefly suggest for each group why this might be the case, using Item C if you wish.   (6 marks)

c) Suggest how a sociologist would collect evidence of racial discrimination in the labour market.   (4 marks)

d) Assess the view in Item E that there is a 'dual labour market' using the data from here and elsewhere if necessary.   (10 marks)